The Wilderness of the North Pacific Coast Islands

The Montague Island Bear

See page 81

THE WILDERNESS OF THE NORTH PACIFIC COAST ISLANDS

A HUNTER'S EXPERIENCES WHILE
SEARCHING FOR WAPITI, BEARS, AND CARIBOU ON THE LARGER
COAST ISLANDS OF BRITISH COLUMBIA AND ALASKA

BY

CHARLES SHELDON
AUTHOR OF "THE WILDERNESS OF THE UPPER YUKON"

ILLUSTRATED

NEW YORK
CHARLES SCRIBNER'S SONS
1912

To

MRS. DEAN SAGE

PREFACE

WITH one exception, the trips described in this book were incidental to others in the Yukon Territory and Alaska. From journals, carefully written at the end of each day, I have tried to reproduce an exact picture of the experiences of a hunter in the wilderness of the large islands visited. The narrative, however, is not a copy of my journals, and may be read independently of the marginal dates, which are inserted merely for the convenience of those interested in fixing accurately the dates of recorded events.

This is a tale of hunting, during rain and storm, for special animals; much of the country traversed was unknown in detail to white men, some of it had not even been trodden by natives; it was not possible to obtain guides familiar with the habits and haunts of the animals; and the time which could be spared for each trip was limited. Little attention, therefore, could be given to natural history which, in the regions visited, has fortunately to some extent been investigated. But no literature, giving the detailed experiences of hunting in all of these islands, exists.

My thanks are due to some of my friends for helpful criticism of the Montague Island narrative, and I am very much indebted to Dr. C. Hart Merriam for numerous suggestions in regard to this part of the narrative, all of which have been adopted.

No one except myself, however, is responsible for any of the opinions expressed in the narrative.

Owing to the state of the weather and the character of the country hunted on Vancouver Island, I was unable to take successful photographs, and I must also thank Charles Camsell, of Ottawa, for sending me some photographs taken by a member of the Canadian Geological Survey, and J. H. McGregor, of Victoria, for some prints of the region in which I hunted the wapiti. The U. S. Biological Survey has kindly permitted me to reproduce some of its photographs; the U. S. Geological Survey also sent a few photographs for reproduction. Francis Kermode, Curator of the Provincial Museum of British Columbia, and Charles Harrison, of Massett, Queen Charlotte Islands, gave me valuable information about the caribou of Graham Island.

I must especially acknowledge the sympathetic interest of the artist, Carl Rungius, in preparing illustrations for the narrative.

The only rifle I used was a Mannlicher, .256 calibre.

Appendices giving a description of the Montague Island bear and some notes on its habits have been added to the narrative; and also a technical description of the caribou of Graham Island, by Dr. C. Hart Merriam, to whom I am much indebted for preparing it especially for this volume.

The most interesting animals occurring in the coast region of Alaska are the big brown bears. Dr. C. Hart Merriam has, for many years, been studying not only the classification, but also the life histories of the bears

of North America. At last he is about to reach con-
clusions on their classification, and in the near future
will publish a book on American bears, which will be
the first instalment of his monumental work on North
American mammals. The monograph on the bears
will be comprehensive and replete with details of their
habits. We await, with eager anticipation, this forth-
coming publication on such a fascinating subject, which
will contain a discussion of the species of the bears
which were the objects of some of the hunting described in this book.

New York, *April* 1, 1911.

CONTENTS

xi

CONTENTS

ILLUSTRATIONS

Vignette on cover from a drawing by Carl Rungius

xiii

ILLUSTRATIONS

XV

MAPS

HUNTING THE WAPITI ON VANCOUVER ISLAND, 1904

.

"Among the scenes which are deeply impressed on my mind, none exceed in sublimity the primeval forests undefaced by the hand of man . . . temples filled with the varied productions of the God of Nature: . . . no one can stand in these solitudes unmoved, and not feel that there is more in man than the mere breath of his body."

—DARWIN.

Wapiti in the Forest of Vancouver Island

CHAPTER I

THE TRIP TO THE MAHATTA RIVER

THROUGH the summer and early fall of 1904 I had been hunting mountain-sheep among the Rockies of the Yukon Territory, and on my return stopped at Victoria for the purpose of arranging a trip for wapiti, *Cervus occidentalis*, during the month of November. Although many sportsmen had killed this fine animal on the island, little had been recorded about it, and nowhere had I seen a detailed description of the experiences of a hunter in the Vancouver Island forests. Some question had arisen as to the exact status of the wapiti isolated there, and the main object of my trip was to secure a bull for the Biological Survey in Washington, so that its relation to the wapiti, *Cervus roosevelti*, of the Olympics could be positively determined. Warburton Pike, who had passed the summer hunting in the Stikine River region and had joined me on the steamer at Wrangel, took great interest in my proposed trip, and through his kind assistance in Victoria I was enabled to make my plans.

The vicinity of Kuyuquot Sound had up to this time been a favorite hunting-ground, as guides could be employed there who knew the local haunts of the animal; but since no steamer started for the section until late in November, I could not wait so long. Pike introduced me to J. H. McGregor, of Victoria, who had

3

recently surveyed timber lands near the mouth of the Mahatta River in Quatsino Sound, and his suggestion that I should hunt wapiti there, where he had seen abundant signs of them all summer, was accepted. McGregor assisted me in every way; gave me a map of the region covered by his survey, and secured for me an assistant, A. I. Robertson, a young Englishman, who had been a member of the surveying party and knew the trail from a point in Quatsino Sound to the river. Throughout the trip Robertson, besides being a congenial companion, proved a most excellent man, and did everything possible to make the expedition a success. Francis Kermode, curator of the museum in Victoria, wanted a cow wapiti for exhibition, and gave me a permit to kill one.

On the night of November 1, during a continuous rain-storm, I sailed on the steamer *Tees* up the east coast and landed at Hardy Bay at 2 A. M., November 3. Some time before a town site had been laid out in Hardy Bay and a trail had been cut twelve miles through the forest to Quatsino Sound; but the town had failed to materialize and was only represented by a trading-store, kept by A. Lyon, for the purpose of supplying the Indians scattered near by along the coast. We slept in his house, and that same morning engaged his brother-in-law, a half-breed Indian—a tall, powerful fellow, who spoke English well and the native language fluently, but knew nothing about the district where I intended to hunt. We also secured an Indian to take an extra pack across the trail. We lost that day waiting on the storm, which still continued, but on

the second morning, although the rain still fell heavily,
I succeeded in inducing our Indians to start. We were
soon rowed across the bay and entered the gloomy,
dripping forest at nine in the morning.

November 4.—The trail, fairly well cut out, wet,
slippery, and muddy, passed over some ridges, wound
around others, led through swamps, and crossed numerous swollen streams. Thoroughly soaked, we arrived
at the east arm of Quatsino Sound in five hours. While
crossing on the trail, the Indian who was in front saw
a deer, which ran off before I could come up. I now
took the lead, and before long, being half a mile ahead,
sat down to rest, depositing my pack near me and
standing my rifle against a stump a few feet away from
where I was sitting. After a short time Robertson
joined me and took a seat at my left. While we
were chatting, a loud crack suddenly sounded directly
behind us, and my companion, shouting "Look out!"
jumped up. I rose with appropriate haste and looking back saw a large dead tree five feet in diameter
falling directly toward me. Springing to one side, I
luckily escaped a death blow as the tree struck with a
crash in the exact spot where I had been sitting; it
broke into several pieces, the branches covering my
pack and nearly striking my rifle. Had I been alone,
or had not Robertson, who was familiar with the sounds
and the dangers of that forest, shouted in time, I would
undoubtedly have been killed. In the mighty forests
of Vancouver Island these big trees constantly fall in
wind or in calm, and one always takes chances when
among them.

At the end of the trail lived an old Kentuckian, Sharp

by name, who had a large house and garden. Several deer carcasses were hanging near, also the skin and skull of a wolf which I obtained for the Biological Survey. After dinner we sent the Indian back, rented for the trip a boat which could be rowed or sailed, and, having waited a short time for a favorable tide, resumed our journey. We rowed through Quatsino Narrows, passed Hotée, the village of the Koskimo Indians, and reached the trading-store of H. O. Bergh in Quatsino village— if a few houses scattered at long distances along the shore can be called a village—at nine in the evening. Here we passed the night.

Quatsino consists of eight or a dozen Scandinavian families induced to locate there by the British Columbian Government, which, following a policy of planting agricultural communities, has given to each family an area of land. These Scandinavians, however, attempt little farming, and agricultural development has been wholly neglected for mineral prospecting. Some of them had found copper in the northeast arm of the sound and had sold the prospects at some profit. Already considerable capital had been invested in a copper property at Yreka.

November 5.—Early the next morning we purchased provisions for the trip and started for the mouth of a creek eight miles distant, where there was a trail which had been blazed by the surveyors through the woods to the Mahatta River, near which we intended to camp.

The wapiti, *Cervus occidentalis,* occurs everywhere in the forests of Vancouver Island, decreasing in numbers southward to within thirty miles of Victoria, in which area but few range. They keep well back from settled districts, and are quite scarce near the east coast and the adjacent woods. They are most abundant in the north end of the island, particularly in the northwestern section and the vicinity of Kuyuquot Sound. Living in

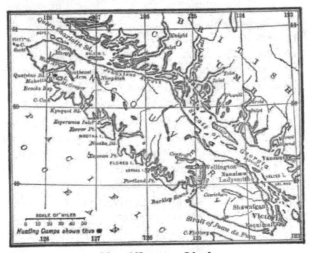

Map of Vancouver Island.

the dense forest they feed on some of the weeds and grasses and browse on the leaves of the salmon-berry, *Rubus spectabilis*, and those of the huckleberry, *Vaccinium*. I saw but few signs high on the mountains or near the tops of the higher ridges; they seem to wander on the lower slopes, in the marshes, along the rivers or near the lakes, and sometimes near the beaches.

The wapiti are seldom hunted by the Indians, who prefer the more easy task of killing deer on the beaches.

They have not been much sought for by sportsmen, who have only hunted in the more accessible places. The natural difficulties of the sport will keep all but the most ardent hunters away, and those who undertake it will not go far from the coast or rivers navigable by canoe. As most of the interior of the island is still unexplored the wapiti have not been disturbed there at all. Protected by dense forests and rough mountains, inconspicuous in the heavy undergrowth and timber, the wapiti will probably roam on Vancouver Island long after those of the United States have become extinct. They had already begun to be slaughtered for their teeth in Kuyuquot Sound, but the government has since taken active steps to prevent it. I could not help thinking that had our bison found some similar refuge to which they could have adapted themselves, much larger numbers would be alive to-day.

. The Columbian black-tail deer, *Odocoileus columbianus*, is everywhere abundant all over the island.* Natives and whites kill it at any time, "jacking" along the beach or otherwise, without any respect for law. Wolves, *Canis subsp.*(?), and cougars, *Felis olympus*, are plentiful; also black bears, *Ursus subsp.*(?), wolverines, *Gulo luscus*, raccoons, *Procyon pacifica*, and red squirrels, *Scuirus hudsonius vancouverensis*. In some places beavers, *Castor canadensis leucodontus*, are common, as well as land otters, *Lutra canadensis pacifica*, minks, *Lutreola vison nesolestes*, weasels, *Putorius streatori*, and martens, *Mustela caurina*. Neither foxes, por-

---

* See " Report on a Collection of Birds and Mammals from Vancouver Island," by Harry S. Swarth, " University of California Publications in Zoology," vol. 10, no. 1, pp. 1-124, Feb. 13, 1912.

The forest of Vancouver Island.

cupines, nor rabbits exist on the island. Three kinds of mice, *Peromyscus, Evotomys, Microtus,* and a shrew, *Sorex vancouverensis,* are abundant.*

During the month of November, bird life, except that of the aquatic birds, which were in great numbers, was scarce. The little western winter wren, running along the logs and dodging about the tangled brushwood, nearly always my companion, was perhaps the most common bird. Bald eagles were numerous in the bays and along the rivers. I also observed a few hawks and pygmy owls and now and then heard the tap of a woodpecker.

The forests of the island are particularly dense and consist mostly of gigantic cedar, spruce, fir, hemlock, and balsam trees. It is only in exceptional areas, here and there in heavy timber, that the ground is not covered with a thick growth of sallal, *Gaultheria shallon,* salmon-berry, and huckleberry. Willows, poplars, birches, and alders grow along the banks of the rivers. In numerous places all this growth is wellnigh impenetrable, and since, in addition, the whole interior is filled with vast swamps, unfordable creeks and rivers, continuous tangles of great logs and fallen trees, it was the most difficult and heart-breaking country that I had ever tramped over.

The surface of the country is a jumble of rough mountains, irregular steep ridges, hills, valleys, ravines, and canyons. Near the coast and bordering the rivers it is more rolling. In the northern part of the island few of the mountains rise above timber line, and during

---

* The scientific nomenclature of some of these mammals, pending a careful revision of the groups, is uncertain.

the almost continuous rains in the fall their slopes and those of the ridges are streaked with white dashing cataracts, and from a distance present the appearance of being lined with broad strips of snow.   The month of November has the heaviest rainfall of the year—rain, storm, and fog almost continually.   The water is so abruptly precipitated that after each heavy rain the creeks and rivers rise to a flood, which subsides a few hours after the rain slackens.   In November the woods are so full of mist that the sight of a rifle is not visible before eight o'clock except on the rare occasion of a clear day.   It is always too dark to see the sight after 4.30 in the afternoon.   I tested this nearly every day, and only once could I see my sights after 4.30 in the afternoon.   Without thorough familiarity with the local landmarks only experienced woodsmen can escape getting lost when away from the main river courses; even with a compass the novice finds it most difficult to keep a course, since ridges and swamps have to be circled if one travels but a few miles in any direction.

When I was there, the woods were so damp and wet that a fire could only be obtained by searching for and finding large dead trees which were fairly sound, and then felling and splitting them to a depth where the damp had not penetrated.   Pitch wood was very scarce, and except at camp, where a large supply of kindling was made and kept dry, it required a long time to make a fire large enough to boil water.

Having left Quatsino village behind us we rowed for an hour through a landscape of mist-covered green hills and mountains.   It was calm and warm, and the air

The interior of Vancouver Island.
Photograph by courtesy of Charles Camsell.

was laden with a strong salt perfume. Then came the wind and with it a drenching rain. We put up the sail and more rapidly sped along. The sound was full of water-fowl, and numerous flocks of geese were flying low, while some were feeding in the bays; great flocks of gulls and terns were screaming in the coves and at the mouths of the creeks. The heads of seals were popping up in every direction, and a school of small black whales were sporting and blowing along our course.

Reaching the mouth of a large creek near the blazed trail, we found two Koskimo Indians who, together with their squaws, were occupying a loosely constructed house which they had erected, and catching and drying dog salmon which were then running up the creek. They were also killing deer and coons every night along the beach. Our tent was soon pitched and I went in the house to visit the Indians.

The Koskimo tribe of the Kwakiutl Indians, then reduced to about twenty families, had sunk into the most depraved state, perhaps, of any of the Indian tribes in the island. They had never permitted missionaries to come among them, and had been plied with whiskey by the traders in spite of seeming vigilance on the part of the authorities.

One of the Indians occupying the house was called Tom—a villanous-looking fellow—and his squaw was coarse and debauched. Far more interesting were Monkey, a short, squarely built man, and his squaw, a medicine-woman who was really picturesque, with a pure Indian type of face. All welcomed me as they sat about a fire in the centre of the room and roasted large clams, which I found to be most palatable. Dried and drying salmon hung on the smoky walls; several coon-skins, stretched on frames, were scattered about, and fleas swarmed. Hunt, the half-breed, soon came in to interpret for me, but our hosts could give no information about wapiti or the country away from the coast. It is so easy for the Indians of Vancouver Island to procure food by fishing and shooting deer on the beaches that very few ever go back into the woods, and then only for a short distance to trap along the rivers. A liberal offer of money did not at first tempt them to assist in taking our packs four miles over to the Mahatta River.

Hearing a loud, splashing noise in the creek, made by thousands of dog salmon which were then running up, I took a lantern and went to the mouth of the stream, where a startling sight was before me. The creek, not over fifty feet wide and very shallow, resembled a solid black mass in aggravated motion. It was literally choked with struggling fish, which were so jammed at the more narrow mouth that many were being forced out of the water, on to the gravel bars on either side.

November 7.—The rain poured down all night and continued through the next day. But in spite of the downpour, Hunt and I decided to make a reconnoissance, and started over the blazed trail preparatory to going forward with the packs the day following. For a mile the trail led along the creek, where the stench of dead and decaying salmon, lying in hundreds on the banks and caught among the driftwood tangles, was almost unendurable. The whole creek was alive with

Quatsino Sound.   November 6.

Quatsino Sound.   Valley of Mahatta River in centre.
Photograph by courtesy of J. H. McGregor.

them, swimming about and forcing themselves up the riffles, while the pools and eddies, their bottoms strewn with eggs, were filled with spawning fish which were quarrelling and fighting.

The sight brought reflections on some of nature's laws—not wholly those of "tooth and claw"—which every year impel so many billions of the several varieties of these noble fish, male and female, blindly to force their way, often for thousands of miles, up swift rivers, small and large, until, wounded and bruised, those which survive succeed in spawning and perpetuating the race. Immediately after they die. Not one survives. Can there be any greater tragedy in nature?

While following the blazes I first realized the difficulties before me. Everywhere the surface was covered with a thick undergrowth of sallal and salmonberry, and the ground was so broken and uneven, so filled with logs and tangled brush, that progress was not only painfully slow, but the vision was so obstructed that I could see through the woods only a very short distance, and then indistinctly. Fortunately, when in Victoria, I had had hobnailed soles put on my leather moccasins. Footgear with hobnails is a necessity, for one must walk on great slippery logs, over fallen trees, and up and down steep hills and ridges. Throughout the trip I wore the ordinary hunting-clothes that I had worn all summer in the Yukon Territory.

About a hundred yards from the bank of the creek, we came to a spot where a black bear had been carrying the salmon it had caught—eating the whole of each except tail, fins, and skeleton. There were several dozen fresh skeletons scattered about, and five or six of them I thought had been cleaned the night before.

In a meandering course the trail followed the side of a ridge rising above a deep ravine through which the creek flowed, and we followed it to a low divide, on the other side of which the waters flowed to the Mahatta River. Deer tracks, some of them fresh, were everywhere, but old wapiti tracks were first seen on and beyond this divide. Finally we descended a steep ridge and proceeded a quarter of a mile to the Mahatta River, then swollen to a torrent, to the spot where we were to make our camp.

This river, deep in places, is from seventy-five to one hundred and fifty feet wide, and races in an abrupt descent its entire length, rushing through a canyon a short distance below the spot where our camp was to be made, and flowing on to Quatsino Sound, three miles below. Its length is only eight miles or perhaps a little more, and it flows in a northeasterly direction from its source in a lake—Lake McGregor I named it—which is about two miles long and half a mile wide. As far as I could learn, no white man had ever been to this lake, and on my return to Quatsino the Norwegians asked if it was true that such a lake existed. Later, when in Victoria, Mr. McGregor, who had run a survey two miles up the river from that camp, told me that he had heard Indian rumors of the lake, but had doubted them. Three miles up from camp a large branch enters the river, flowing from a ridge to the southeast, which with the southwest arm of Quatsino Sound forms the divide. Another large branch enters half a mile farther up. It has its rise in a ridge to the west, on the other side of which the waters flow to Klaskimo Inlet, on the west coast.

At frequent intervals huge trees had fallen across the river in such a way as to form bridges on which it was reasonably easy to cross; in other places, on sharp curves or shoals, or near anything which served as a barrier, great log-jams had formed, where a tangle of broken tree branches and even rocks had accumulated.

The most fortunate thing that happened in the whole trip was the finding of pitch wood close to the camp, sufficient in quantity to last us all the time we were there.

We walked down the river to the canyon, and then climbed to the tops of the high ridges on the right. Only deer tracks were seen high up; those of the wapiti were below. Descending we swung around toward the blazes and followed them until after four in the afternoon, when they were lost in the darkness, which descended before we realized it. I had caught my direction in time by compass, and slipping and falling in the darkness we stumbled along the ridge side until we reached the shore, when the barking of the Indians' dogs guided us a quarter of a mile through a dense sallal thicket to the tent. The Indians were out "jacking" for deer and coons, and after watching the squaws as they made baskets of cedar-bark strips I slept while the rain beat against the canvas. I had seen enough to know that the chance of finding a bull wapiti in those woods was not encouraging.

CHAPTER II

HUNTING WAPITI ON THE LOWER MAHATTA

November 8.—The Indians had returned about 2 A. M. with a fine buck, a doe, and two coons, all killed on the beach. In the morning, after buying the skulls for the Biological Survey, I tried to persuade them to take packs over to the Mahatta River, but they refused. Fortunately it stopped raining and remained cloudy and misty the rest of the day. I paid them for the skulls, offered them slightly more to carry the packs, and the sight of money aroused their avarice to such an extent that both agreed to go.

About nine, while the others were making up the loads, I started ahead to spend the day hunting alone. Proceeding along the trail I noticed that the same bear had eaten two more salmon during the night, and soon I saw a fresh deer's track in the trail. Advancing very slowly, stopping every few steps to listen, I followed along the ridge over the divide to where it slopes precipitously to the Mahatta River, a quarter of a mile from the point where we were to make our camp. There I stopped to listen, and after a few minutes thought I heard a stick crack somewhere below. More attentively I strained my hearing to catch a sound, and, sure enough, after a few moments another stick cracked. Creeping forward I saw four wapiti cows feeding well down on the hill-side, while the wind was

16

blowing directly from them to me. Fortunately, the forest on that part of the slope was fairly clear. They were cropping weeds and browsing on the salmon-berry leaves. As they were slowly working upward toward me I waited for fully fifteen minutes, in the hope that a bull might appear near them. They moved about without the slightest noise except that now and then one would crack a small stick, and not once did they seem suspicious or on the alert.

Finally, assured that no bull was near, I determined to take that chance to secure one of these animals for the Victoria Museum, and at the same time to provide meat for our camp. Since the largest cow was then near the top, a hundred yards away, I moved a few feet forward to a clear line of space as she faced me, and fired full into her chest. She turned, staggered a few steps, and fell dead, while the others went trotting off downhill. It was 1 p. m., and I circled about the ridge for two hours on the chance of finding a bull, but did not see one. Returning to the carcass I tried to photograph it. The animal had fallen between logs and brush in such a way that I could not stretch the carcass for measuring, and it would have required so much time to handle it alone that I could not have skinned it before dark. After making the cuts and skinning the hind-quarters, I hurried to camp and brought Hunt back to help me. The skin was off about dark, and taking the head and the liver we stumbled to the tent, where, after supper, I spent two hours preparing and salting the skin. The Indians had returned to their camp.

The rain had begun to fall before we slept, but now

that a cow wapiti had been so quickly and easily killed I felt much encouraged in regard to the prospect of finding a bull. There was one disappointment—the knowledge that I could not indulge my love of hunting alone. The day's experience forced me to realize that Hunt must accompany me while hunting, since the hours of daylight were so short that if an animal were killed in the afternoon at a distance from camp it would be impossible for me alone to take off the skin and bring it back before dark. Wolves and ravens were so abundant that the skin would be mutilated if left on the carcass in the woods overnight.

During the whole of my stay on Vancouver Island it was not cold enough for a frost except on the tops of the higher mountains, and the residents said that it was usually as cold in November as in any of the winter months. The rain and damp, however, had a thoroughly chilling effect, which was more penetrating than the cold of a dry climate like that in the interior of the Yukon Territory.

November 9.—In the morning Hunt and I started up the east side of the river. Though it was cloudy, no rain fell and we tramped about the thick woods and through swamps all day, and having crossed the river on a log, we returned to camp on the other side. Old wapiti tracks and dung were abundant, but we did not see any that were fresh. Robertson had gone back over the trail for more provisions, and on his return had also brought in a good supply of wapiti meat. There was a small stove in the tent; plenty of wood had been prepared; the ground was hard and level, and we

"She turned, staggered a few steps, and fell dead." November 8.

CALIFOR

were fairly comfortable. As we dozed off to sleep it began to pour and continued to do so until early next morning.

November 10.—The whole of that day was cloudy, but at times the sun would break through and shine for a short while. Crossing the river, we climbed to the top of a ridge and kept going from ridge to ridge all day. There were no tracks in the higher country except those of deer. In a beautiful level area, where the woods were fairly free from undergrowth, in the midst of gigantic spruce and hemlock trees, we stopped for lunch and made tea. The sun broke through the clouds, bestowing its genial warmth and casting great long shadows all about, while its rays gave a sparkle to the watery sallal leaves. The forest, deep and silent, assumed a grandeur hitherto unsuspected, and I realized the possibilities it would offer to one tramping about in it during the summer months, when the rain is not so continuous.

We shortly reached a point from which it was necessary to turn toward camp if we were to arrive there by dark. Descending diagonally, we encountered a swamp of sallal so dense that it was just possible to force ourselves through. A small creek flowed across it toward the slope, down which it rushed in precipitous descent, in some places almost in water-falls. What was my surprise to see in the quiet waters above the slope, near the top of the ridge, numerous coho salmon from eighteen to twenty inches long! I would have been surprised to see even a trout up there, and would not have believed it possible for those salmon to have worked up so high. Hunt, who was familiar with the habits of the various species of salmon on the Pacific Coast, told me that cohos were famous for wriggling up small streams to places almost incredible. In the swamp we saw many places along the creek where a bear had been eating these salmon, leaving the usual remains—fins, tail, and bones.

We kept on descending and circling about the ridges, while the fog became dense, until Hunt, thoroughly confused in his directions, insisted that my compass was out of order and was not pointing correctly; but I had learned that lesson before, and had more faith in it than in him. He soon declined to follow me and took his own course, thinking that he would strike camp in a direction that I knew would lead him farther up river, when we were already three miles above the tent. I descended alone to the lower country, and there found numerous wapiti tracks, but all old except one of a cow, which had been made within two or three days. I reached the river about a mile above camp and waited for Hunt, knowing that he would soon find his mistake when he saw the current flowing in a direction the reverse of that he had insisted upon when we had separated. While near the river I heard the notes of water-ouzels. These, together with the chatter of red squirrels, the song of the winter wren, and the cry of the bald eagles along the river, were the common sounds of life heard about the woods. After Hunt had joined me without making any excuse for his error or receiving any comment from me, and while we were walking on the river-bank just before dark, the mournful howl of a wolf made the woods echo in the direction of the wapiti carcass. It continued at intervals until we slept. All summer I had been in the wilds of the interior of the Yukon Territory without once hearing the voices of the larger animals, and those dismal wails, pealing out of the dark, gloomy forest in the night, were fascinating to hear.

November 11.—We crossed the river early the next morning, to continue the hunt on the lower levels as far as daylight would permit. It rained for three hours in the middle of the day and was cloudy and foggy during the remainder. All day, between the pauses to listen, we walked slowly and cautiously, but no fresh wapiti tracks were seen except those of a cow and calf two and a half miles above the forks. There we crossed on a log and returned toward camp. The wolves were again howling near the carcass, which later we visited and found untouched. I had begun to feel somewhat encouraged about the weather, but, judging by the wapiti signs and the difficulty of walking and seeing in the thick brush, the prospect of finding a bull was doubtful. That night it began to rain, and not again during my stay, except for one day, was the sky clear, nor except once or twice for a few moments did the rain cease falling day or night.

November 12.—I was anxious to go off alone, and the next morning decided to hunt in the section of the country lying toward the southeast. As we were rising a sharp and continuous chatter sounded high up in a tree about sixty feet behind the tent, indicating that two birds were fighting, and Hunt, who was nearest the entrance, ran out, and I followed. The noise of the chatter rapidly descended to the ground, and Hunt, running into the brush, came back to meet me with two struggling birds in his hand—a red-breasted sapsucker, *Sphyrapicus ruber nootkensis*, still screeching and pecking at a tiny California pygmy owl, *Glaucidium gnoma californicum*, which had its beak fastened in the shoulder of the sapsucker. The owl had struck it high up in the tree and both had fallen fluttering to the ground, nor had the owl released its hold when Hunt handed them to me. Later that night I took off their skins.

Again alone, I felt the charm of tramping in the dripping woods, in spite of the heavy rain. Crossing first some high rolling hills and then a dense salmon-berry swamp, I came to some foot-hills at the base of a mountain where the trees were large and the forest was impressive. Stopping every moment to look and listen —I could not hear well in the downpour of rain—I proceeded step by step until I saw a pretty doe standing and watching me not a hundred feet away. Slowly advancing to within fifty feet I watched the graceful creature for fifteen minutes as she stood innocently gazing at me. When I started on, she began to walk slowly away and soon disappeared in the brush. After advancing a short distance and looking ahead I saw another doe with a fawn standing among some high ferns and watching me. Surely, I began to feel that this great forest had a mysterious fascination, singular and unique, and quite different from that of the high wilderness of the interior, where, all summer, I had wandered in the sunshine among mountain peaks and

valleys, viewing vast landscapes stretched out before
me. Here, in this majestic forest, dark, lonely, and
wild, I felt a companionship with those lithe deer
watching almost trustfully my intrusion into their
densely wooded recess, yet walking off slowly and timidly, as if they did not know me quite well enough to
admit me to terms of intimacy.

The rain increased, the fog settled more densely, but
I continued circling about, now through thick brush,
now over ground carpeted with wet, spongy moss, sometimes passing over slippery logs lodged across small
ravines, often wading through a boggy swamp, until at
last, entering some heavy timber, I came upon fairly
fresh tracks of a small band of cow wapiti, not more than
five or six, so far as I could judge, that had been feeding all about that vicinity. I tramped over the foot-hills
near, but, not finding any wapiti, was obliged to start
back. The fog was then so dense that I could see but a
few yards in any direction, and taking out my compass
set a course and followed it. After a sufficient time,
when I did not reach the salmon-berry swamp that had
been crossed earlier in the day, I felt sure that something was wrong, and examining my compass carefully
discovered that the water had so penetrated it as to
make the needle stick at a certain point. As a result it
had been guiding me in a direction opposite to the camp.
After vigorously shaking it I soon found the right
course, hastened my steps, and reached the swamp as
it began to grow dark. Some of the salmon-berry
bushes in Vancouver Island grow ten feet high and their
branches, barbed the entire length, shoot out in all

directions, so that unless one can see clearly and thus
avoid them, they constantly strike the face and endan-
ger the eyes.   Gradually, however, I forced my way
through and at dark came to the river, a short distance above camp.   The wapiti tracks in the area I had
tramped over that day offered some encouragement, and
I determined to take Hunt with me on the next and
go higher on the ridges in the same direction.

November 13.—The next morning was spent tramping
over the higher country, where there were no wapiti
tracks at all, and in the afternoon we travelled over the
flat country nearer the river, where old tracks were
abundant.   Rain, rain, rain, fog, and mists—that was
all.

November 14.—The next day, after rapidly passing
through the flat country and reaching the east branch
two and a half miles above camp, we climbed the high
ridges that extend parallel with it, tramped along the
tops and on the slopes, but saw only deer tracks.   Descending to the branch, the rain was pouring down so
hard that we found it had risen over its banks and had
flooded the flat area on each side for a hundred yards
back.   After wading about for some time, a log on
which we could cross was found, and going to the other
side we went to the main river and later returned to
camp.   All over the lower country, particularly near
the river and its branches, old wapiti tracks were abundant.   I was at last convinced that in that part of the
island at least the wapiti does not roam in the higher
altitudes; for we had not once seen even old signs there
—only deer tracks.

Travelling through the forest of Vancouver Island.
Photograph by courtesy of Charles Camsell.

Sunshine in the forest of Vancouver Island.
Photograph by courtesy of Charles Camsell.

CHAPTER III

HUNTING WAPITI ON THE UPPER MAHATTA

November 15.—It thundered continually all that night and in several places not far from our tent we heard trees falling and large limbs breaking and tearing through the branches. The river was running very high and roared as it swept by our tent. I had decided to make a camp three miles up river at the forks, from which point the country beyond could be more conveniently hunted. In the morning Hunt, Robertson, and I took some provisions, a sheet of canvas, my rubber blanket, and a few other necessities, and brought all to the forks.

A hundred feet below the junction of the forks the river curved in a sharp bend, practically enclosing a small flat area extending about two hundred feet back to a high terrace which, like the chord of a circle, isolated this low piece of land in the river bend. The space, occupying an acre and a half, was two feet above the river and covered with a fine growth of gigantic spruce trees. Along the foot of the terrace was a depression which indicated a former river-bed. Just at the curve several large logs had lodged across the river, and these were jammed with trees and dead wood, about which the current fiercely eddied and swirled as it broke through with a roar. Twenty feet from the old river-bed and parallel with it was a big water-soaked spruce

25

log five feet in diameter. In the heavy rain we constructed a shelter against this and facing the terrace. The canvas and rubber blanket, tied together, were thrown over inclined poles, and the sides of this shelter were filled in with heavy brush until we were satisfied that it would withstand rain and storm.

Our new dwelling being arranged for, Robertson returned to the main camp, that our new home might be left as quiet as possible. Hunt and I were now alone, but before starting a fire we went out and hunted about the woods near by, to anticipate if possible any animal that might be frightened away later by smoke or noise in the camp. Farther up along the river we saw several regular fording-places made by wapiti in descending the steep banks—special fords always recognizable by the deep paths which were cut to the roots of the trees. Returning to our quarters at dark we started a fire against the log, and soon a clam-shaped hollow was burned out, which would glow red exactly like charcoal and reflect the heat into the shelter.

November 16.—As the rain did not penetrate the shelter we were comfortable. The next day was worse then any which had preceded—wind, hail, rain, and fog. Yet we tramped all day, up the east branch and about the adjacent woods, without seeing a fresh track. Not finding suitable wood we could not even get a fire for tea. Every creature had sought shelter from the fierce elements—not even the little winter wren, which up to that time had appeared in spite of rain, was about. Shortly after our arrival at camp we had a big fire burning; our clothes were hung under the shelter, and the

glorious heat which the log reflected gave inconceivable
comfort after the cold drenching we had been exposed
to all day. It was a satisfaction to feel that we could
thus defeat the rain, which continued to beat all night
on the canvas above us.

November 17.—The rain fell steadily through the next
day. We started up the east bank of the main river
and walked back and forth between it and the foot-hills
situated a mile back. It was cheerful to see again the
winter wren flitting about and bursting out in occasional song. Once a spike-buck jumped up, ran a short
distance on the top of a hill, and stood looking at us.
The buck was about to rut and its horns were clear
of velvet. Though the wapiti meat was spoiled, I did
not mar the pretty sight by yielding to Hunt's eager
urging that I should kill it. It circled a few steps, came
a little nearer, and lifted its foreleg in a curve as it
watched us, as if it wanted to gain a better acquaintance with the strange intruders. As we advanced, it
walked on noiselessly a few steps and paused to look
at us, then continued retreating and stopping until we
passed it and came in the wind, when its tail went up
and it trotted down the other side of the hill out of sight.

Old wapiti tracks were numerous everywhere below,
but none were seen as we went higher. At noon we
halted in a little ravine by the side of a small brook
which came dashing in little cascades over a steep slope.
There we made tea and then advanced diagonally in the
direction of the river across a more level country filled
with salmon-berry and huckleberry bushes, until a break
appearing ahead in the woods indicated a lake. The

surface of the ground was flooded for two hundred yards back into the woods, and alternately wading and walking on logs, we finally reached the submerged shore of the lake.

I climbed a tree inclined out over the lake and beheld a pretty expanse of water extending between high ridges on both sides. After days of travelling about in the dim forest, where the vision was continually obscured, it was a relief to look once again over space. The hills rose so abruptly at the upper end that I knew the lake was fed by precipitation from the surrounding ridges, and that it was the true source of the Mahatta River. We were near the lake's lower end, and waded back to the dry land, cautiously proceeding to where the Mahatta River flowed from the lake. It emerged in a large volume about a hundred feet wide, racing in abrupt descent. There we saw the fresh tracks of a cow wapiti and those of her calf, both leading down the river and close to the bank. I was in the lead, walking ahead as cautiously as possible in the thick, high brush, and in a few moments saw a cow wapiti standing motionless about a hundred feet away with ears pricked up and looking a little to the left of my line of approach. Motioning to Hunt to stop, I also remained still, and as the cow slowly turned and began to browse on salmonberry leaves I saw another approaching her, and in straining my eyes to see a bull, discovered still another cow. In a moment, as a short trumpet-like bellow sounded a few yards beyond those in sight, a whole band of wapiti began to run toward the river, and I discerned indistinctly several forms hurrying through the brush.

A section of forest near the Mahatta River.
Photograph by courtesy of J. H. McGregor.

Lake McGregor.
Photograph by courtesy of J. H. McGregor.

I heard them then plunging into the rushing waters of
the river as I ran toward it, and arriving on the bank
saw nine cows and four calves quickly wading across,
quite indifferent to the force of the swift current. In
midstream all turned, ears erect, facing me in curiosity,
while one after another kept trumpeting as the racing
water surged against their sides without disturbing
them in the least. While, in a perfectly straight line up
and down the river, they continued to stand looking at
us for ten minutes, I pushed my kodak through the
bushes and snapped it three times. But the lens was
covered with a film of moisture and no pictures resulted.

We remained quietly watching those graceful animals standing in the torrent against a background of
big trees and little suspecting how completely they
were at my mercy. Whispering to Hunt how fortunate it was that they were not thus innocently standing before Indians instead of ourselves, he remarked:
"Yes, an Indian would shoot every one of them." I
knew that his Indian nature was boiling also, and that
he was aching to have me begin a slaughter. Finally,
after continual trumpeting, they slowly waded to the
opposite shore, where they again turned and looked at
us for a few moments, until an old cow indifferently
walked off into the woods, followed by the others, which
were soon lost to sight among the brush. My keen
pleasure in that fascinating sight of wapiti life in the
grim forest as the rain was pouring down was more than
neutralized by not having found a bull with them.

Since it was nearly four o'clock, and camp was three
miles down the river, we began to walk as rapidly as

possible.   After going a hundred yards my eye caught a glimpse of something suspicious in the woods across the river, and pausing, I finally recognized two of the cows standing motionless and watching us.   So perfectly did they blend with the brush and foliage that had it not been for the peculiar look of their ears I could not have seen them; as it was, I could not make Hunt recognize them for a long time.   But we were obliged to hasten; the woods were already growing dark, and in ten minutes I could not see my rifle-sights; a little later the ground was not visible and there was inky blackness in the woods, while the rain increased.   The moon was full and there was a glow of light in the dense clouds above, but as none of it penetrated the forest, we had to cut stakes and feel our way, guided by the noise of the river.   The next three hours brought a trying experience.   Step by step we felt our way, now crawling over logs, now working through tangled masses of dead timber, now crossing swamps and always protecting our faces from low limbs and brush, until we reached the east branch of the river, where we found the water so high that it was rushing over the log on which we had expected to cross to our camp.   It was somewhat discouraging to be obliged again to grope along the bank for a quarter of a mile until we found a log high enough for a crossing.   Though quite exhausted we were shortly under shelter, and a roaring fire, food, and tea soon put us in a more cheerful state of mind. Ere long we slept soundly, while the rain still poured.

November 18.—In the morning we crossed the river and zigzagged back and forth between the slopes of the ridges and the flat country below in the hope of seeing a bull. There was a hard rain-storm all day, while the woods were filled with fog, which made them dark and gloomy. Soon after starting we saw a doe, which, like other deer I had seen, stood and looked at us with curiosity and did not move away until we had approached very near to her.

In the forest of Vancouver Island in November the sight of any kind of an animal was always stimulating and cheerful. When the rain slackened red squirrels were always abundant and continually enlivened my spirits by chattering in the trees, while the repeated sight of them, skipping about on the ground and approaching me for the seeming purpose of scolding at my intrusion, dispelled the profound loneliness induced by the dripping woods. But when the rain increased to a downpour, even the squirrels sought shelter, and the occasional sight of a deer or cow wapiti was the only evidence of life in the dismal environment.

We persisted in forcing our way through the brush, which grows much more densely on that side of the river, until we reached the lake, when it was so late that we crossed the river and hastened back. No fresh wapiti tracks were seen and even old ones, except in the vicinity of the lake, were scarce. Before reaching camp, just at dark, the wind and rain had increased to such an extent that we were shivering with cold and had great difficulty in getting a fire, since all the wood which had been cut was so thoroughly soaked that it was necessary to fell a tree in the dark and then chop and split it—a long and harrowing task. In such weather the outlook for finding a bull wapiti was most discouraging, and particularly so because the section of country along the west branch was the only remaining territory not investigated which was available to hunt from our present camp. The steamer was due to arrive in Quatsino November 23, and would not return until a month later. Therefore time could not be spared to move camp up to the lake and hunt the country beyond.

The wind kept increasing and the rain fairly poured as we lay down to sleep on that wild, never-to-be-forgotten night. The wind soon developed into a fierce southeast gale, which was said by the inhabitants to have been the severest that had swept over the north end of the island in years. The rain fell in sheets and, driven by the wind, beat loudly against the canvas and sifted in at the sides. Our shelter, likely to collapse at any moment, trembled, and for several hours we remained awake from sheer dread and nervousness. Outside all was inky blackness, and the river roared loudly as the wind, coming again and again in shrieking blasts, drove the rain against the canvas. On all sides, and often near the camp, great trees were crashing down with a frightful noise, while all about us, with each blast of wind, big limbs broke and fell, ripping through the branches, some of them striking the ground close to our shelter. We could hear falling trees strike the river with loud splashes, while others, carried down by the current, lodged against the jam, where the roar of the impeded flood continually increased. The spot for the shelter had been carefully selected; no dead trees were near save one enormous spruce which, inclining toward

it, could not have been avoided. At every violent rush
of wind, strewing its path with crashing trees and falling branches, we shuddered, thinking of that great tree
near us. Yet, at last, as the waters rushed and roared,
as the floating trees boomed against the jam on the
curve, as the darkness resounded with the noise of falling timber, while the wind, charged with torrents of
rain, whistled and shrieked and the shelter threaten-
ingly trembled, we dozed off into a nervous sleep.

November 19.—But I had not long lost consciousness
when I felt a grasp on my shoulder as Hunt exclaimed
that we were being flooded. Sure enough, water was
running through the foot of the shelter, and rapidly rising, while we heard a flood of water rushing through the
old river-bed directly in front near the terrace. We
were then isolated from the higher land and the water
was roaring on all sides of us. Hunt lit a candle and
held it protected while I quickly hung on the poles of
the shelter my rifle, rücksack, clothes, a few provisions
and other things, after which we waded to the log and
climbed up on it. We were both in our underclothes,
and although there were dead limbs protruding so that
we could hold on to them, we soon became so cold that
it did not seem possible to endure it. We did not know
the hour; the trees were still falling and the storm
raged unabated; the water soon rose three feet on the
log and swept by, surging among the trees. At every
blast of wind it was difficult to hold ourselves on the log,
yet we realized that the only chance for life was to remain there and trust to the flood subsiding before rising
high enough to sweep us off. Finally we had become so

numb that we were only able to hold ourselves on the log by winding our arms around the branches.

After an hour the water had risen three and a half feet on the log, but it was rising more slowly than at first. The roar at the jam which had dammed the waters and caused the flood came in tremendous volume through the darkness—an ominous foreboding of the fate that might be pending. Another hour passed before the dawn enabled us to distinguish the trees, and shortly after we noticed an elevation of land near the lower end of the log. The water had then fallen two or more feet. The day before, Robertson had brought up a good supply of pitch wood, and by the rarest luck had wedged it among the dead limbs protruding from the top of the log. We crept forward and seized it, waded to the little island and lighted it; then, chopping off the dead branches of the log, we threw them on the burning pitch wood and made tea and drank great quantities of it until we revived enough to wade to the wood supply and increase the fire.

Soon everything was visible, and it was startling to see the water rushing by, eddying and swirling among the trees, while the jam appeared like a huge waterfall. With daylight, though the wind continued, the rain stopped pouring, and the water rapidly lowered, not more than a foot passing through the shelter. That soon disappeared. The fire, transferred to its old place against the log, was coaxed into a large blaze, and we prepared to dry clothes and blankets under that little shelter which had withstood wind, rain, and flood.

All about, strewing the surface in every direction,

were great fallen trees and standing splintered trunks; the ground was covered with broken branches and all the standing trees were ragged, scarred, and gashed. The scene of forest destruction before our eyes was made more impressive by the fearful roaring of the surging river torrent which was sweeping by, carrying trees, branches, logs, and driftwood, which were lodged against the jam. When, later in the day, the river fell to the water-mark which I had made at the time we erected the shelter, I found that during the night the water had risen six feet eight and a half inches.

The wind continued all day, and soon the rain increased so much that I decided not to attempt hunting, but to remain about camp and dry everything before the fire. Hunt went down to the main camp for provisions, and did not meet Robertson, who was coming up somewhat in doubt as to how we had passed through the storm. After Hunt returned, we decided to hunt the following day and then to return as quickly as possible to Quatsino in order to make sure of the steamer.

During the day large flocks of ducks, seeking shelter from the storm, flew by, and numbers of bald eagles collected along the river and kept flying up and down, continually uttering their shrill screams.

November 20.—Once more Hunt and I slept profoundly in that little patched shelter, and at daylight started up the west branch, or more accurately the southwest branch. We soon forced our way through the tangled, barbed bushes of a salmon-berry swamp and emerged into a fine area of heavy forest which was quite free from undergrowth as far as the ridges, half a mile beyond. The rain fell all day, sometimes very hard; but once the sun suddenly broke through the clouds, and the wet brush sparkling among impressive shadows tantalized me with the thought of how fascinating these forest scenes must be when sunlight is a familiar guest. It soon disappeared behind dark clouds and the rain-drops again began to patter on the foliage. Wapiti tracks, some of them fresh, were numerous everywhere, and I redoubled my caution, stopping every few steps to look and listen, seeking and climbing every high log to obtain a wider view through the woods, and zigzagging back and forth between the ridges and the river. About a mile up, the branch divides in two large streams of equal volume, and we followed the one flowing from the south. Just above the forks it flows from long, high mountain ridges through a gorge for two miles in a succession of cataracts and water-falls.

After circling back from the gorge, as I was slowly approaching the river just above the first waterfall, my eye suddenly caught the body of a large wapiti not a hundred feet away, its head completely obscured by the foliage of salmon-berry and sallal. Instantly cocking my rifle and holding it to my shoulder I waited, exulting in the thought that a bull was before me, so near and so well exposed that he was already mine. After a moment its head came up, but how intense was my disappointment to see that of a very large cow! As I stood motionless, parts of the body of another were visible through the foliage beyond, and I waited eagerly for three minutes, hoping to see a bull. The nearer cow then suddenly began to walk toward me, carrying her head in such a way that I knew she had scented me, and after two or three steps she was joined by two other cows and a calf. All stood for a moment on the bank looking in my direction, and then noiselessly crossed the river and silently disappeared in the woods. No bull appeared.

We went on with renewed interest and unabated caution, circling about the rolling country and over the ridges beyond, where this fork of the branch rushes in cascades down through another deep canyon. As we ascended, old wapiti tracks continued numerous, and the sallal increased in abundance and became more dense. I should have liked to follow this fork up to its source in a lake which, judging by the volume of water flowing at so high an elevation, evidently exists, but it would only have been possible by moving camp near the high ridges. We were obliged to return, and reaching camp at dark, slept for the last time under the shelter.

November 21.—In the morning I left Hunt to pack up the material and bring it to the main camp, and started alone to circle the ridges northeast and thus take a last chance to run across a bull. I went through the deep woods on the flat, and just before arriving at the foot of the ridge saw a small buck deer approaching. He soon saw me, stopped a moment, and then with springy steps advanced, sniffing in curiosity. He was beginning to rut, and I stood motionless as he slowly approached, holding his head forward to get my scent. When within twenty feet of me the odor struck his nostrils; he threw up his tail, turned and trotted away, but kept stopping at intervals to look back, until he disappeared. I went along the slope of the ridge and came to the place where the fresh tracks of cow wapiti had formerly been observed, but none were to be seen. I saw a doe noiselessly stealing away, but pausing again and again to look back at me. Circling about the divide I crossed a vast salmon-berry swamp and saw nothing but old wapiti tracks on the other side, and there, taking a compass course, I started toward camp.

Reaching the carcass of the wapiti I was surprised to see it had been untouched by the wolves, though ravens were flying about it and quarrelling. It had been left on its back with one hind leg and two forelegs sticking high up, so that the appearance presented was somewhat startling—perhaps enough so to make the wolves cautious. Just at dark I reached camp, and Robertson, who had taken a load over to the beach, told me that the Indians had been badly frightened by the storm, several trees having fallen close to their cabin. A wild spectacle the woods presented after that storm! Here and there large areas had been completely devastated of trees, which had fallen in tangled masses in every direction; the whole forest was mutilated.

November 22.—We slept in the woods near the rushing river for the last time, and in the morning I started ahead on the remote possibility of seeing a wapiti on the trail. That day it did not rain and the sun ushered me from the woods of Vancouver Island and made the beads of water on the trees and foliage glitter as it

bathed the forest with bright warm shafts of light. Red
squirrels skipped about and chattered, and little winter wrens were flitting about in the brush. I walked
slowly along a trail, then so obstructed by fallen trees
that often wide détours had to be made to pass around
them, never relaxing my caution, always looking for the
coveted bull. Soon after midday I reached the beach,
and the others joined me an hour later.

Tom and his squaw were just leaving in a canoe he
had recently fashioned from a single log of spruce.
Monkey decided to remain and go over to our camp for
the empty bottles and whatever else we had left behind.
The salmon were still crowding up the mouth of the
creek, and I was interested to see Monkey's small mon-
grel bitch, not over fifteen pounds in weight, swim out
and grab a weak salmon of ten or more pounds by the
centre fin and, in spite of its struggling, swim back to
the bank and drag it upon the beach. After procuring
the skulls of minks and coons which the Indians had
accumulated during our absence, and taking bread and
tea, we loaded the boat and started for Quatsino, but
not without my feeling a deep reluctance.

The mysterious fascination pervading those dim,
gloomy woods had captured me. In spite of the rain
and fog, wind and storm, that vast majestic forest in its
impressive solitude had cast a spell upon me. One
soon becomes familiar with it, learns how to tramp
through it to the best advantage and absorb its beauties. In the rainy month of November it is steeped in
almost continual gloom which, together with fog and
rain, give to it a wild loneliness full of charm and quite

unique. Walking about with constant stealth and eager anticipation, pausing to look and listen every few steps, now seeing a lithe deer stealing away in the dark, dripping foliage, now looking at the white, foamy cascades dashing down the steep slopes; again, after the disheartening toil of forcing oneself through a swamp, enjoying the sudden contrast of the clear areas beneath gigantic trees, and the wonderful effect of sunshine filtering through them; watching red squirrels chatter with satisfaction and tiny wrens flit about in joyous life; and withal suddenly beholding the wapiti silently browsing among the dense foliage and mysteriously blending with the dark forest—the experience deeply impresses him who loves nature's primitive wilderness. But this is only one phase of its all-pervading charm.

Had I been there earlier, during the rut of the wapiti, the chances for finding bulls and killing one would have been better. But in November they had separated from the cows and had withdrawn into the deep recesses of the forest—where I cannot say, nor could I learn. Whether they feed singly or in bands or seek other parts of the island, or whether they had been overlooked in the areas I had hunted, remains to be ascertained. Neither Indians nor white residents of the region could give me any information about their habits.

The buck deer were then wandering in the day time nearer the beaches, and as we were rowing along the shore among the screaming gulls, honking geese, and flying water-fowl, I saw one standing near in the sallal. An hour after dark we arrived at Bergh's, and hearing

"Monkey" and his squaw.   November 23.

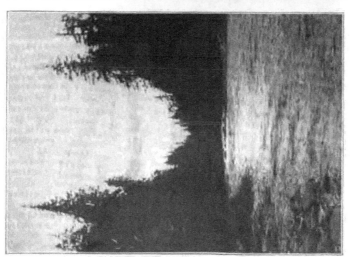

The Mahatta River.

Photograph by courtesy of J. H. McGregor.

that the Koskimo Indians were dancing in their village two miles above, Hunt, a Norwegian, and myself rowed over there after supper. We entered a large wooden communal house, where there was a wild orgy. Indians, some of them stark naked, were sitting and lying about the fires, chatting with the squaws. Others were drunk, and all were painted or wearing huge grotesque masks, while at intervals they would rise and jump about at the end of the structure in a weird dance.

It began to rain and continued to do so until the small steamer *Queen City* arrived, early in the morning, November 24. Hunt left us to return to Port Hardy. He had been a most willing and faithful man, though deficient as a hunter and lacking in ability to find his way in the woods.

November 24.—We steamed through Quatsino Sound to Winter Harbor, a small village situated at the entrance, and after a stop went out in a heavy sea to sail 350 miles down the west coast to Victoria. After three hours a gale was blowing and the captain put back again to Winter Harbor, where we remained until four the next morning, when the sea had subsided enough for another attempt. The coast was obscured by a dense fog and at one in the afternoon we reached Kuyoquot Sound, where I made arrangements with a hunter named Donohue to secure a bull wapiti for the Biological Survey. Later he sent one to Washington, but I never learned where or when he killed it, or where bull wapiti are to be found in November.

The next day we reached Clayoquot Sound, where we were obliged to remain for twenty-four hours. It is very dangerous for a small steamer to run down the west coast in the fall, and the captains take no chances whatever, but once in a harbor they do not proceed to the next until the sea is favorable.   We left Clayoquot about noon and sailed under reduced steam pressure.   The sun was out and the coast was clear.   Lofty ranges of verdure-clad mountains, often breaking into high cliffs which fall into the very sea, rise abruptly from the rock-bound shore, beyond which huge reefs and small rocky islands extend several miles out into the water.   The waves breaking against the rugged coast carry with them a continuous border of foam as they creep up and down the cliffs, while the sea, surging and dashing over the reefs, spots the whole surface white for miles out from the shore.   Truly the sail down the west coast of Vancouver Island is one of the most picturesque south of the Alaska coast; it would be a constant joy to coast along in the bright, calm weather of summer and behold its beauties as the sea foams white around its reefs and dashes against its rocks and cliffs.

We entered the Alberni Canal in the night, and on the morning of November 28 beheld the magnificent snow summits of the Olympics, opposite the lowland coast of Vancouver Island on our left.   The sight of them awakened anew thoughts of the lordly wapiti which ranges so abundantly in their forests, but the appearance of distant smoke and spires made me realize that my free untrammelled life in the wilderness—a life I had been indulging in since early summer—was ended, and at one in the afternoon the steamer docked at Vic-

Findlayson Arm penetrating Vancouver Island.

toria. It had required four and a half days to make the 350 miles from Quatsino to Victoria.

I took the boat for Seattle that night and remained there for two days, when I boarded the train and reached New York on December 5.

HUNTING THE BIG BEAR ON MONTAGUE ISLAND, 1905

The Bear nursing her Cub on Montague Island

See page 109

CALIFORNIA

... nursing her but on ... ... Island

See page 88

CHAPTER IV

HINCHINBROOK ISLAND.

At five o'clock on the afternoon of April 13, 1905, I sailed from Seattle on board the steamship *Portland*. My destination was Montague Island, which stretches in a northeasterly direction across the entrance to Prince William Sound. My mission was the study of a great unknown bear said to inhabit the island, but of which no specimen had as yet reached any museum.

No problem in the natural history of the game animals of America is more interesting, or presents more difficulties, than that of the coast bears of Alaska. Dr. C. Hart Merriam is inclined to the opinion that the coast region of Alaska, from the Alaskan Peninsula easterly to and beyond Yakutat Bay, is the centre of distribution of the big bears of America—the area in which the various species of brown bears originated and from which the ancestors of the grizzly radiated. The material from this region thus far collected and studied shows an unusual range of individual variation, and also a surprisingly large number of well-developed species. But lack of well-authenticated specimens leaves so many questions in doubt that, after a discussion with Dr. Merriam, and by his advice, I selected Montague Island as a field for hunting, to add, if possible, my quota of assistance toward clearing up this question.

For a long time I had been eagerly anticipating a trip in the month of May among the rugged coast ranges of Alaska—a trip to be devoted exclusively to hunting the bear. No sight in the American wilderness is so suggestive of its wild charm as that of the huge bear meandering on the mountain-side, or walking on the river-bank, or threading the deep forest. He who still retains his love for wild nature, though accustomed to the sight of wild animals, and surfeited in some degree with the killing of them, feels a lack in the wilderness—perhaps the loss of its very essence —when, tramping about in it, he knows that the bear, that former denizen of its depths, is there no more— exterminated forever.

The magnificent grizzly of California is practically extinct, and it is now too late to secure specimens for comparative study. Already, in most parts of the Rocky Mountains south of Yellowstone Park, the sight of a grizzly is a mere chance. Its numbers are rapidly diminishing also in Mexico and southern British Columbia, and even the black bear, in some of the large areas formerly frequented by it, has become so scarce that sportsmen no longer attempt to look for it. The process of extermination is rapidly going on all along the Alaska coast, and the fine large brown bears, in spite of the present law, are, I think, doomed to become scarce, if not extinct, before increasing travel and population. Already the grand bear of Kadiak Island—that great beast, the largest of its genus in the world—is rarely seen.

Determined, therefore, to assist in securing material

for study, I found myself on the way to Montague Island, but without any definite idea of how to get there or how to hunt. No traveller or hunter had been in its vicinity without being told that on Montague Island the bears were so numerous and fierce that they immediately drove off everybody who attempted to land. I had learned of several doubtful methods of reaching the island, and finally accepted the suggestion of Mr. O. J. Humphrey, of Seattle, who advised me to go to Nuchek, on Hinchinbrook Island, where Charles Swanson, who had a trading-post to supply natives living at that village, could perhaps assist me in crossing to Montague and provide me with reliable men.

April 14.—On the morning of April 14 I awoke to find a calm, beautiful, mild day, and the boat steaming up the coast of Vancouver Island. My eyes and soul were gladdened by the landscape of green forests, inviting mountains, dashing white cataracts, and the snowy ranges of the mainland. During the whole voyage, until my arrival at Nuchek, April 21, there was scarcely a cloud in the sky; no winds stronger than light breezes swept the ocean; the days were warm and balmy; the sea calm, almost without a swell. We steamed up the lovely inland channel, stopped at Ketchican and Juneau, and the following night dropped anchor in the picturesque harbor of Sitka, nestled in high, rugged mountains still buried in the winter's snow. The nights had been clear and bright under the full moon, and it was enchanting to walk on deck —the pale light glinting over the smooth water, the dusky, timbered slopes rising abruptly from the fiord, those nearer appearing as huge dark shadows lined above by white, those more distant, on the mainland, so blended below with darkness that the serried, peaked, snowy crests above, all aglow in the moonlight, seemed mysteriously suspended in the heavens. I could look ahead, as the prow of the steamer ploughed through the sparkling stream of silvery water, directly in the path of the moon's reflection, and could see the cataracts dashing perpendicularly down the mountain side, gleaming and sparkling against the dark shadowy background, while beyond appeared those glowing white mountain crests suspended in the sky. One pleasant feature was missing from this delightful voyage. The preceding fall, when I had sailed over the same course as far as Juneau, great numbers of gulls had continually followed the steamer, gracefully soaring about it, and at intervals swooping with plaintive screams to eat refuse thrown on the water. Also, numerous ducks were seen both in flight and swimming on the surface. But in April all these were absent, preparing to breed.

April 18.—The two hours' stop at Sitka afforded a change and recreation, and I fell asleep as the steamer was raising anchor, to awake opposite the magnificent Fairweather range, the white tip of Mount St. Elias just visible in the distance. The broad expanse of the ocean was to the west. I could not attempt to describe the grandeur of that sail on a calm, clear day, facing this wonderful mountain range, perhaps one of the grandest stretches of mountain scenery in the world. Among those who have felt its sublimity is John Burroughs, who mentions it in his charming narrative of the Harriman expedition. Gulls became more numerous; schools of porpoises were leaping about and leading the bow; whales were rising and blowing in every direction; and now and then a fur seal was seen as it appeared in a long leap out of the water. All day, across a glassy sea, the vision was exalted by this vast mountain range, rising abruptly from an apparently level green strip below, with mighty glacier after glacier filling the valleys, extending over plains, reaching in places to the very sea. Under towering Mount St. Elias we stopped at Yakutat late in the afternoon, when the boat was immediately filled with Indians anxious to sell their tourist stock to interested passengers. We remained there several hours.

The next morning, St. Elias appeared far distant to the southeast; the day was the same, and we coasted along opposite the St. Elias range until we stopped at Kayak Island at seven. Soon after leaving, I saw in the distance, like a white line of snow on the horizon, the mountain crests of Montague Island. It was my last night on the steamer, and eagerly as I anticipated reaching my goal, it was not without regret that I realized that the voyage was at an end. The passengers, nearly all from Cook Inlet, now returning for the summer, had been most congenial, and many of them had spent years in the country. They had volunteered plenty of advice about the Montague Island bears, most of which confirmed the reputation of these animals as I had heard it, and some was also full of caution as to the dangers of bear-hunting; but a few persons of experience and common-sense expressed doubt as to my being able to find any bears at all.

April 21.—The steamer was dropping anchor when I was called at 3.30 A. M. and found all my provisions and outfit on deck. A boat was lowered, and I was rowed through the darkness to the sleeping village of Nuchek, where my outfit and I were landed on the beach. The boat returned, and soon the *Portland* steamed off.

Swanson had gone in his schooner to Ellamar, not to return for several days. But his wife, a sweet, pretty Russian woman, kindly offered to take care of me, and at once aroused two natives, who brought all my effects into the old trading-store, and I was soon in Mrs. Swanson's house, surrounded by her five children, with a breakfast before me. During all my stay in Nuchek, Mrs. Swanson was most kind and hospitable, as was her husband later, and before leaving I became greatly attached to them.

As it was soon daylight, I could look about. The village of Nuchek consisted of thirty or forty small wooden houses occupied by the natives, an old trading-house constructed many years ago by the Russians, a little church with a low-pointed spire, and a larger house occupied by Swanson; all situated on a hill at the entrance to Port Etches. The land is a bog through which paths have been made among the huts by gravel brought up from the beach.

Hinchinbrook Island was first noticed by Cook, who, on May 12, 1778, named it Cape Hinchinbrook.

In 1779, two Spanish boats, under the command of Ignacio Arteaga, probably anchored in Nuchek Bay. A boat was sent out to ascertain whether the shore connected with the mainland, and upon the return of the officer, who reported it to be an island, Arteaga promptly took possession of it in the usual form.

In 1783, Potap Zaïkof was commander of a Russian expedition consisting of three boats, which set out from Unalaska in search of trading-grounds to the eastward. In September these three boats remained in Nuchek harbor. Zaïkof sent out a party, evidently in the direction of Prince William Sound, to investigate the trading conditions. This party had much fighting with the natives, and later was obliged to go into winter quarters in a bay on the north end of Montague Island, now called Zaïkof Bay. Here they endured many hardships; scurvy broke out among them, and by spring nearly half of their number had perished. Those who were left set sail for the Aleutian Islands, never to return.

In 1787, Portlock spent nearly a month, parts of June and July, in Nuchek harbor, when he made a chart of the bay and named it Port Etches. He also ascertained that the adjacent land was an island. In 1787 and 1788, expeditions of Spaniards and of Russians were cruising about Prince William Sound, and some of these touched at Nuchek. Martinez, a Spaniard, entered Zaïkof Bay in 1788, and found there the log house occupied by Zaïkof's party four years before. The trading-station, now the village of Nuchek, was founded by the Lebedif-Lastochkin Company in 1792, and became the main base for trading to the eastward. Cook had found natives living there, but Vancouver, who visited it in 1794, reported that there were none inhabiting the island at that time. Within a few years, the Lebedif-Lastochkin Company failed, and later Nuchek was occupied by the Russian-American Company, which kept agents there until Alaska was transferred to the United States, from which time to the present, different individuals have kept up the trading-post.

This in brief outline is the early history of Hinchinbrook Island, and the founding of Nuchek, which, from the beginning, has been the only inhabited spot on that island.

The trading-store was then owned by Charles Swanson, who furnished supplies to the natives in return for the skins of the sea-otter and the land-otter. Including women and children, there were about 130 natives in the village. A Russian priest had his headquarters there, but spent most of his time elsewhere visiting the natives about Prince William Sound, and was, I believe, more actively engaged in collecting furs than souls. Below the village is a long sand beach, connecting the entrance to Port Etches with the high mountains which rise abruptly from the west coast, a mile and a half distant. There is a broad bay in the front, Cape Hinchinbrook is visible to the east, covering perhaps an acre, and in the centre of the bay are three groups of high rocks, their perpendicular walls rising from the water to a height of fifty feet. Being familiar with the fact that one hundred and sixteen years before Cook had sent out a boat from the *Resolution* to shoot some of the white birds flying about these rocks, it was interesting to see still the same sight, for the rocks were white with gulls about to breed. The whole of Hinchinbrook Island is mountainous and, in appearance, partakes strictly of the character of the mainland. Large bears* of a species unknown before my visit are fairly abundant on the island, also shrews, three species of mice, weasels, minks, marmots, a few silver foxes, cross-foxes, and land-otters. The red fox is seldom seen, and there are no red squirrels.

The natives are the easternmost branch of the Innuit stock, Chugachigmiuts, as Dr. Dall calls them. They have the appearance of true Eskimo, in spite of an infusion of Russian blood. As a whole, they are now an unhealthy, degenerate lot, nearly all afflicted with tuberculosis. Though the women still bear children abundantly, the tribe is decreasing in numbers. Converted to the forms of the Greek church, they are well under the influence of the priest. When in Nuchek, they live in cabins, and during the early summer subsist chiefly on cod and halibut. Later, they catch and dry salmon, which last for part of the winter, and for the remaining months eke out an existence as best they can, mostly going in debt to Swanson. They hunt sea-otters in the summer, and trap land-otters in the winter. Each family has one of the seal-skin boats, the bidarka. With the exception of seal mukluks worn on

* Only one skull of this bear—that of a mature male—has been received by Dr. Merriam. It has some unique characters which, if they hold on other skulls of the Hinchinbrook bear, are sufficient to separate the bear as a new species.

the feet, they now wear the clothes of the white man. They are a lazy, improvident lot, and, like most of the natives, both on the coast and in the interior, make an effort only under necessity.

April 25.—I slept on the floor of the ancient store-house, a cold, damp, inhospitable place that had never been heated. The next day I made the acquaintance of one of the northeast storms of that region, for a gale set in, with rain and snow, which continued for three days and spent itself on the fourth, leaving the whole country white. I could do nothing but remain in the house during the day and sleep in the store at night. After the storm cleared, I took my rod and cast for a while in a small lake near by, with no result other than one small trout. I spent the afternoon walking about the woods, seeing only a few birds—ravens, crows, jays, and sparrows.

The next day was showery, and the following morning, Thursday, Swanson returned. He said he could give me two natives and a bidarka, and take me over to Montague Island in his schooner. But since the natives would not go until after the Russian Easter week, we could not start until the following Tuesday. The storm soon returned and continued until I left Nuchek.

It did not, however, prevent the natives from preparing for Easter, and at twelve, on Saturday night, the noise made by the firing of every rifle in the village roused me. The church bell began to ring and, worked by relays of children, continued without ceasing until twelve Sunday night. The priest was away, but the natives remained in the church until 4 A. M., and re-

turned to it, between intervals of feasting, all through
the day. Early Monday morning the bell began to
ring again, continuing to do so until twelve Monday
night; then came a repetition of the church-going and
feasting, until all were gorged almost to the point of
illness. But at last Easter was over. I was to start
the following day; and notwithstanding Swanson's report of the scarcity of bears in Montague Island—he
having seen only two in all the years he had cruised
about there—I was eagerly looking forward to the pleasure of again being in camp.

Swanson, a large fine-looking man of generous im-
pulses, had spent many years on the Alaska coast, and
for the last twelve had been established at Nuchek, depending for his living upon the sea-otter skins brought
to him by the Nuchek natives.

As the early romance of Canada and the West was
linked with the beaver, so that of Alaska is linked with
the sea-otter. Its range, which formerly extended from
Bering Sea to the California coast, is now restricted to
the territory between Vancouver Island and the Aleutian chain. It is exceedingly scarce south of the latitude of Prince William Sound, and now is not common
anywhere. The fragmentary information given me by
Swanson seems worth recording. This refers wholly
to the present habits of the sea-otter in the vicinity of
Swanson's hunting territory about Hinchinbrook and
Montague Islands, and the tributary feeding-grounds,
where he had had excellent opportunities to observe
the habits of this animal. I transcribe literally from
my notes:

"Sea-otters have young any month in the year; Swanson has seen them in all seasons with young of the same age. The female otter gives birth to only one pup, and, lying on her back in the water, carries it on her breast. When it is old enough to be fed, she breaks clams and shell-fish with her teeth and inserts the food in the young one's mouth. When she dives for food, she leaves the young one on top of the water. The pup must be six months old to feed itself, and stays with the mother for a year. Sea-otters feed on clams, crabs, sea-urchins, mussels, kelp, and shell-fish, diving from five to thirty fathoms or more to get them. They range for feeding about sixty miles. They have special feeding-grounds in shallow water, on "banks" or near the shore, and feed at night. In the day they go off shore, often thirty miles or more, and sleep. They seem to have well-defined ranges over which they feed, and, though they may be temporarily driven away by too much hunting, sooner or later they return to the familiar feeding-ground. Swanson was uncertain as to how often they feed, but the native chief of the hunters told me it was only one day in two or three—I am inclined to think he himself is not certain.

"Sea-otters always travel by swimming on top of the water, on their sides, back, or belly, and sometimes seem to leap along. Formerly they went into inlets; now they always remain outside. In rough and heavy weather they come close to shore, often in the surf, where they play, lying on their backs, jumping, turning somersaults, chasing each other, and racing. In calm weather they are never seen playing. When one is seen, it is usually sleeping. Natives say they have seen four or five sleeping at the same time. Often several—sometimes as many as forty—have been seen together, and when so congregated they are never asleep. When sleeping, one of these animals looks like a black drift stick with its extremities out of water. The head and hind flippers are always a little out, the body submerged. They cannot stay under water for more than five minutes without coming up to breathe. Their vision is like that of a seal, their ears and nose very keen. Being very shy, they are afraid of whales and sea-lions, and always leave when those mammals are around. Swanson has several times tried to keep the young alive, but soon they refuse to eat and starve to death. The fur is equally good through the whole year. Sometimes, especially in August, an old otter will have an inch of fat on it.

"Later, I discussed all these points with the native chief of the hunters, who added nothing, and verified all, so far as he could understand me, except that he affirmed that the sea-otter does not hear well, while Swanson insists that it does. They are steadily decreasing; males and females are killed in about even numbers.

"To hunt them successfully the weather must be calm, the sea smooth, and without much swell. Under such conditions the natives can hunt them at any time of the year. Outside of Prince William Sound, June and July are the best months. At other times the weather is so uncertain that the natives do not venture out hunting, except to make an occasional attempt during the latter part of April and May. From eight to ten bidarkas is the best number for a hunting party. If there are less than eight, the chances are proportionately less; if more than ten, two parties are usually made up. Two natives must always be in a bidarka, and it is better to have three. The reason is, that speed, sustained by steady paddling, is needed, and when an otter is seen, the man ahead must stop and hold his rifle ready to shoot while the others paddle. Only the head man shoots, and if he must keep paddling, his hand and aim become unsteady.

"The natives know the feeding-grounds. Sometimes they paddle off shore to these and remain there all night, so as to be on the spot early, as soon as they can see. More often they camp on shore, and leave in time to reach the feeding-grounds by 3 A. M., often having to paddle ten or more miles to do so. There is always a chief of the hunters, appointed by Swanson, who directs the hunt. They form the bidarkas in a wide semicircle, and then advance, keeping a sharp lookout for the sleeping or swimming otter. These natives have a remarkably keen vision to detect and discriminate objects in the water. As soon as one of them sees an otter, he holds up his paddle and points until it is seen by all; then the boats advance toward it, trying to close the circle. When an otter first realizes the existence of danger, it raises its head to look, and sometimes rises quite high out of water. Then it dives and swims two or three hundred yards. All paddle rapidly in the direction in which they think the otter has taken, for they can usually tell its course by the way it bends as it goes down. As soon as it comes up to breathe, one or two shoot, to keep it down, while the others continue paddling and closing the circle. The otter keeps coming up, each time more out of breath, nearer and nearer some of the bidarkas, more and more quickly driven down by repeated shots. The circle grows small and smaller, until, gasping for breath, the hunted animal must rise high out of water—sometimes two feet—and recover for a moment. Now is the chance for a favorable shot, usually delivered by the man in the bidarka which is nearest to the otter, though often two or more fire at the same time. The natives have Winchester rifles, and are excellent shots at objects in the water.

"Sometimes an otter goes under a bidarka, and, once outside the circle, it usually gets away; sometimes an otter is very cunning and raises only the tip of its nose out of the water to breathe, in which case it may escape, or more likely require a large number of shots to hit it. Swanson has seen more than fifty shots fired to secure one otter. The secret of success, and the most difficult part of the hunt, is to close the circle. When a good circle is made around an otter it seldom escapes. Occasionally it takes seven hours to kill one, but an hour is the average time. In the excitement of the hunt there is constant shooting and rivalry, but, strange to say, the natives seldom shoot one another. When a circle is made around more than one otter, a small proportion, perhaps one, is killed, but the operation is the same, although necessarily more irregular. A female is easily killed if she has a pup, because she

will leave it only to dive, and always come up close
to it. When hit, if not killed immediately, she will
grab the pup and hold it with her fore flippers until
her death convulsions. The young one cannot dive,
and often, after the dead mother has been picked up,
it will swim up to the bidarka and bawl, when it can
easily be taken alive.

"Tributary to Prince William Sound are four widely
separated feeding-grounds of the sea-otter: one off
Point Steele, on the east end of Hinchinbrook Island;
one off Wooded Island, near the southeast corner of
Montague Island; one about midway between that
and Middleton Island, near Wessell Reef; and the
last off Cape St. Elias, on the southwest end of Kayak
Island. The otters killed at this last point are said
to be lighter in fur than those killed at the other places.

"In order to keep the natives hunting, Swanson is
obliged to make the following arrangement: If they
go to Point Steele or Wooded Island, they can paddle
in their bidarkas direct from Nuchek, and may reach
either feeding-ground in from two to seven days, as
the weather permits. If they go to the other places
Swanson carries them, with their bidarkas, in his
schooner, and anchors while they hunt. In any case
he furnishes them, free, half of their provisions, consisting of flour, bacon, sugar, and tea; and for each sea-
otter killed, whatever its quality may be, he pays
them in trade at reasonable prices, or $200 in cash.
The native who kills the otter gets most of the money,
allowing the others only enough to pay for the other
half of their provisions and something extra to the

men in his own boat.   The hunter who sits in the bow
of the bidarka is its owner, and is usually paddled by
his sons or other boys.   The hunters must start out
and hunt as Swanson may direct them.   They usually
keep in debt, as otters have become so scarce that he
can no longer keep even with them, and were it not
for a few land-otters—thirty or forty in the course of
the winter—he would run badly behind.   In 1904
eight sea-otters were killed; in 1905, only three.   The
previous years averaged from eight to fifteen, the number decreasing each year.   It is not likely that Swanson can continue his trading-store, and the natives must
then go to Ellamar to trade their skins, or some time
they may abandon Nuchek altogether."*

* The above notes were written in 1906.   Arthur B. Cooper wrote
me from Cordova, May 10, 1911, that the sea-otter is now very rare in
that region.   They have disappeared from all localities except Point
Steele, where one is rarely observed.   Only about thirty natives remain
at Nuchek, but many of these spend most of their time elsewhere.   Since
my visit there a large number of them have died.   Swanson left in 1907;
there is no trading-store at Nuchek; the natives have abandoned hunting
the sea-otter.

CHAPTER V

MONTAGUE ISLAND

TUESDAY, the second of May, arrived at last, a clear, calm day. In the morning I rearranged and packed my equipment and provisions, which had been brought from Seattle, and all were conveyed aboard the *Olga*, Swanson's schooner, which was anchored in the back bay, near the sand spit. We left, at 2 P. M., to sail around out of the back bay to the entrance of Port Etches, where, from Nuchek Bay in front, we could make directly across to the north end of Montague Island, seven miles distant.

With the assistance of Swanson I had employed two natives: Misha, a veteran of fifty years, who owned the bidarka; and Baranof, a boy of twenty years, who could speak some English, and cook as badly as most Indians. Swanson brought with him in the schooner three other natives with their bidarkas, in the hope that they might see and kill a fur seal or two on the way from Montague Island to Ellamar, where he intended to go after leaving me. One was Sitka, the chief of the sea-otter hunters, a tall, active man, who showed traces of Russian blood for several generations back; the second was one Mark, the most typical of all the natives, formerly the best otter hunter, and one of the few who had killed bears on Montague Island; and the third was his brother Pete, who looked strong and healthy, and was then reputed to be the best otter hunter in the tribe.

Surrounded by high, snow-covered mountains, we sailed down the bay in a light breeze, frightening numerous waterfowl from the water, and gladdened by hearing the spring songs of the sparrows in the trees on the shore near by. Sitka shot at a coot sitting on the water, but just missed it; as it rose to fly, I was surprised to see him kill it on the wing, a sure evidence of the small chances of a sea-otter, should Sitka be in the nearest bidarka. Slowly we drifted through the narrow channels as I trolled, without result, for halibut, and when we came around into the outer bay, the wind died out, so that we had to anchor, being unable to beat against the incoming tide. After two hours, the breezes freshened and we reached the bay opposite Nuchek, to find all the inhabitants of the village assembled on the beach, waving all kinds of colored cloth—a joyful adieu. And a romantic sight it was, with the lofty snow mountains in the background, behind the quaint village graced by the single little church spire. We steered for Montague Island, but progressed slowly in the dying winds, and soon it became evident that we could not reach our destination that night. I therefore stowed myself in a narrow bunk, looking forward with delight to being in the woods, under my own shelter, on the morrow.

May 3.—As the anchor was being lowered at 6.40 A. M., about half way down from Zaïkof Bay, I awoke and came on deck rejoicing to feel that at last I was to land on Montague Island. Two hair seals were seen

out in the bay while we were at breakfast, the only
ones I saw on the whole trip. They are more abundant in winter, when the natives kill them to get skins
for their bidarkas, and also for their boots. The oil
they use for various purposes, and they eat the flesh
with relish.

We were soon ashore, a spot was selected, the shelter put up, all my provisions placed under it, and the
bidarka was stored well up on the beach, after which
we returned to the schooner for lunch. Rain began
to fall, and at once a northeast storm descended in
all its fury, with snow, wind, and squalls. It continued for two days, and was so violent that Swanson
did not dare to raise anchor and go. We stayed
aboard the schooner, with nothing to do but watch
the barometer for a sign of change. The monotony
was broken only by a visit from two American prospectors, who were camped in the bay half a mile below.
They had arrived just before us, having been prospecting along the coast of Hinchinbrook. They intended,
as soon as the weather was favorable, to sail their little sloop down the east coast of Montague to the only
landing near the south end, in the hope of finding
some "ruby sand," which contains gold.

May 5.—On the morning of the third day the storm
relaxed; at noon the rain ceased; Swanson sailed off,
and at last I was before a fire in my own camp. The
camp was on a little knoll in the woods, close to the
water, with a beautiful outlook. In front and on the
left, across the bay, were rolling, snow-covered hills;
on the right, the open sound, and rugged, lofty moun-

tains of the mainland were dimly visible in the distance; behind were the high mountains of Montague Island, plainly to be seen through the large spruce trees. The whole west side of the island was buried under deep snow, with the exception of patches here and there in the woods, which were boggy and covered with thick, soft, green moss. We intended to spend next day in camp, and make final preparations to start for the east coast, where there was less snow and the mountains were more accessible from the shore; then we expected to continue down the coast in the bidarka, hunting at intervals whenever we could land.

It was my purpose to collect what small mammals I could; hence I set some traps for mice in the little trails which completely checkered the surface of the woods, while Misha went across the bay in his bidarka to examine some traps he had set two weeks before for land-otters. Before long he came back, bringing a fine male otter which he had found dead in one of his traps, and immediately skinned it. The skin and skull are now in the collection of the Biological Survey at Washington.

Soon the beautiful little rufous humming-bird came buzzing about the shelter, evidently curious at this intrusion on its domain. Bald eagles were flying overhead and, as I sat under the shelter, a shot sounded from Misha's rifle. Going out, I saw an eagle caught and fluttering on the top of a large spruce tree. It soon died and remained there. I did not show my indignation, realizing that Misha had killed it thinking it would please me.

I was again installed in the wilderness; a sense of
deep contentment stole over me as, a little later, I
sat looking out on the calm water of the beautiful bay
—ducks lazily floating about; geese flying low to their
feeding-grounds, making the air vibrate with the music
of their honking; gulls screaming; large flocks of shore
birds skirting the beaches, while behind, in the woods,
there sounded now and then the sweet song of a war-
bler. The feeling of freedom cast a soothing spell over
me as I fell asleep that night, while rain-drops were
pattering against the canvas. Soundly I slept, to
awake and find the next day perfect.

Visiting my traps, I found two tiny shrews and a
large mouse. The latter proved to be a new species,
and has been described by W. H. Osgood, of the Biological Survey, as *Microtus elymocetes*, one of the largest
species of the genus *Microtus* found in America. After
skinning these small mammals, I sorted out such provisions and parts of my equipment as could be packed
in the limited space of the bidarka, and watched Misha
preparing a *kamlayka* for me. This was nothing but
a seamless cotton shirt, which he rubbed to saturation
with seal-oil, and, after drying it, put on a second coat,
which made it waterproof. This is used when one sits
in a bidarka in the rain or rough weather. It is spread
over the port-hole and fastened down with a string,
thus keeping the water from entering the boat. The
best *kamlaykas* are made from the guts of the bear,
but since the natives at Nuchek seldom kill bears, such
kamlaykas are rarely seen among them.

After lunching I took my rifle and was soon wading

"Behind were the high mountains of Montague Island." May 6.

Misha and Baranof paddling the bidarka. May 6.

through snow and tramping about the woods, crossing the glades, and going high up on the ridges. No bear tracks were seen, and birds were rather scarce, for I saw only jays, a few warblers, chickadees, varied thrushes, and sparrows. In circling to the shore, I came upon the camp of the two prospectors, who received me with hospitality and told me that they had tramped across the island to the east coast without seeing a sign of bears, and they doubted if there were any on the island. Returning to my camp, along the beach, I was soon again enjoying a calm, peaceful evening, gazing out over the water of the bay, which was like glass. I fell asleep early, listening to the music of the honking geese.

I must here interrupt my narrative to give a brief description of Montague Island.

Montague Island, totally uninhabited since Cook first observed and named it, is about fifty miles long, from six to ten miles wide, and stretches in a northeasterly direction toward Hinchinbrook Island. There are smooth beaches nearly everywhere along the west coast, and it is fringed with numerous little islands which, in many places, form protected channels for the navigation of small boats. There are three large bays on the west side, all good harbors. The country extending back from the coast to the mountain ranges is quite flat and heavily timbered, and flowing down from the mountains are about fifteen rivers, all large enough to admit salmon, by every variety of which they are regularly entered.

The east coast is entirely different. At the north end are two large bays, Zaïkof Bay and Rocky Bay, both good harbors. Elsewhere, clear to the south end, the shore is so rock and reef bound, that not even a small sail-boat can find a place to anchor. There are but few places where even a bidarka can land, except at the mouth of the small creeks, falling from the basins, where

Map of Prince William Sound, with Montague and Hinchinbrook Islands.

the running water forms, for a few feet only, a gravel beach. Two or three rugged mountain ranges, running parallel with the coast, traverse the entire length of the island, becoming lower at the south end. These ranges are more distant from the west coast, but approach to within three miles of the east coast, near which, at intervals of from two to three miles, vast

spurs jut out at right angles; in some places their
steep slopes almost overhang the beach. The main
range and spurs, very rugged, are from 1,500 to 2,500
feet high, and show plainly the result of erosion and
glacial moulding.

The country between the coast and the main range
is much broken, and consists of steep hills and rough,
irregular ridges. Between the spurs, where they con-
nect with the main range above timber line, are vast
basins somewhat circular in shape and from two to
three miles wide, though often narrower. These basins,
surrounded by snow-capped mountains, have broad,
rolling, hilly pastures, usually devoid of trees or brush,
with the exception of a stunted spruce here and there.
Often some of the bare hills are very rough and rocky.
Through each basin flows a creek, fed from the snow
above; after emerging it runs through a steep gorge,
and often descends in long water-falls and cascades.
Though resembling one another, each basin has its
own strange, grand, scenic beauty. The slopes of the
mountains around are exceedingly steep, often broken
and precipitate. The mountain crests are covered with
snow all the year round. In many places the slopes
are covered with a thick growth of salmon-berry bush,
growing downward in such manner as to render it
exceedingly difficult to force one's way through it.
Scattered about are stunted spruces and patches of
alder, also sloping downward; but in steep places these
aid the climber, who can grasp the alder for support.

It is in the clear places on the mountain-sides and
basins that bears mostly feed in the month of May.

Except on the steep slopes above the timber, walking is fairly easy, as clear spaces where salmon-berry does not grow can always be found, and devil's-club, though abundant, can easily be avoided. One does not go far from the east coast before he must climb a succession of steep hills and broken ridges, but in the timber all are covered with a thick cushion of green moss, which gives a secure footing. The woods are composed of two kinds of hemlock, *Tsuga mertensiana* (common), and *Tsuga heterophylla;* and two kinds of spruce, *Picea sitchensis* and *Picea mariana.* The last is found mostly in the swampy glades. Most of the underbrush is salmon-berry, *Rubus spectabilis;* huckleberry, *Vaccinium;* alder, *Alnus sitchensis;* and devil's-club, *Echinopanax.* Particularly on the north and west sides, the woods are broken into clear, grassy, boggy glades, usually dotted with small depressions filled with water. On the south end of the island some of the spruce is large and fine, and in Macleod Bay there was already a party cutting it for the Valdez market. In May the entire slopes of the mountains on the west side are covered with snow.

The climate of Montague Island, because of its complete exposure on all sides, is the worst in the whole region; the east side particularly being exposed to the continual northeast storms of April and May, while the west coast receives the gales from the west, which blow more constantly in the winter. The northeast storms descend every week during April and May and last from two to three days. One can hope to get reasonably fair weather only in June and July, but even then it is uncertain. Before Cook's time, and perhaps for a short time afterward, natives, probably Chugat-chigmiuts, dwelt on the west side of the island, as is evidenced by the stone implements and pieces of copper still to be found there.

The only mammals* existing on the island are the Montague Island bear† (*Ursus sheldoni*), land-otter (*Lutra canadensis*), very abundant; field mice (*Microtus elymocetes*), shrews (*Sorex obscurus alascensis*), and marmots (*Marmota caligata*). The mink and weasel, both abundant in Hinchinbrook Island, do not exist on Montague Island. Red foxes (*Vulpes kenaiensis?*) were formerly abundant, but are now practically extinct, as the natives have not seen a track in the winter for over eleven years.

Bird life is abundant, but not in variety. In May, bald eagles are very common, nesting in the big spruce trees along the shore. Owls, rock ptarmigan, water-ouzels, sparrows, thrushes, the rufous humming-bird, stellar jays, a few warblers, winter wrens, crows, and ravens, and a few other varieties are about all the land birds I saw. Water-fowl, including ducks, white-cheeked geese, and shore birds, are there in numbers, and pelagic cormorants, gulls, and black oyster-catchers are particularly abundant. Geese breed there. Spruce grouse, common on Hinchinbrook, do not occur there.

* See "Mammals . . . Birds, of the 1908 Alexander Alaska Expedition," University of California Publications in Zoology. Separate from Vol. 5, Nos. 11 and 12, pp. 321–428. (This is the report of an expedition to Prince William Sound, including a study of the mammals and birds of Montague Island.)

† The bear on Montague Island proved to be a new species. See Appendix.

On the east side, there is only one river, near the south end, in which salmon enter, and only the hump-back and silver salmon run up it. Halibut, cod, and bass are caught anywhere about the island, but the natives do not often seek them, and then only in the calm water of the bays. Scattered all along the coast at intervals, and always at the mouth of a creek, are loose little huts made by the Nuchek natives from hewn plank and driftwood, in which they live while trapping land-otters in the winter. These are called *barrábaras* by white men, *mumduks* by the natives. About thirty or forty land-otters are taken every winter, and each native has his own territory and barrá-baras, which others respect as his exclusive property.

CHAPTER VI

HUNTING THE BIG BEAR

May 7.—During the night the thermometer registered 32°, and it was drizzling in the morning, but nevertheless we packed the bidarka, or rather the natives did, as only they understand how to do it. It could hold only a limited supply besides our blankets. At 7.45 in the morning we started. I occupied the middle port-hole of the three-hole bidarka, which was so shallow and small that I could neither get in nor out without assistance; once inside, I was completely wedged in, and the thought of capsizing was not a pleasant one. The bidarkas of Nuchek are very small compared with those of the Aleut natives. Misha was ahead and carried, inserted under a thong on the outside of the bow, his rifle and spear, which latter is used to fasten to and hold up a seal if one is killed.

Swiftly we glided along, the paddles plying the water first on one side and then on the other, for these natives never paddle in any other way. The calm bay was full of the fantastic, beautiful harlequin ducks, geese were returning from their feeding-grounds near the shore, numerous horned puffins dotted the surface, and on the land itself, varied thrushes and sparrows were singing in the trees. We passed out of the bay and along the rocky east coast, which is full of

75

continuous reefs extending from one to five hundred yards out from shore and, as the swell broke over them, the whole coast as far as I could see was dotted with white foam and spray, up to the irregular white line of breakers on the beach. We dodged among the reefs, slipped through great quantities of sea-weed, everywhere abundant, until noon, when we reached the first barrábara, ten miles down the coast, from which point I was to make my first hunt for bears.

It had cleared, and the day was beautiful and sunny. Immediately after taking a bite to eat, I started with my usual equipment, rifle, field-glasses, and kodak. Most unfortunately, not being familiar with the character of the country I was to traverse, I wore leather moccasins. I started up the creek to reach the basin at its head. Avoiding the devil's-club and salmon-berry bush, climbing up and down the steep hills and ridges, I came to a point where the creek emerges from a deep gorge, above which two streams join, dashing down in beautiful cascades over cliffs several hundred feet high. Beyond was the basin surrounded by mountains, all glistening in the sun. At once I started to climb the south mountain slope at the entrance to the basin, trying to force my way through the thick salmon-berry growth, and for·the first time learning the difficulty of such an undertaking. After a vexatious experience, I reached the clear slope, which was very steep, and soon realized that on the slippery, icy ground my moccasins were totally unfit for walking and indeed very dangerous. Slowly I kept ascending diagonally, perhaps for a thousand

"Above which two streams join, dashing down in beautiful cascades over cliffs several hundred feet high."   May 7.

feet, until I reached the snow line, and paused to enjoy the scenery. Again, at last, I was in an amphitheatre of rugged mountains, extending in a well-defined circle, enclosing the rolling pastures of the basin below, which reached down to the green hills and uneven ridges of the valley. Beyond was the broad ocean, now rocking and sleeping, a vast expanse, with its white border of breakers distinctly sounding on the beach. A bald eagle was soaring above me in evident curiosity, rock ptarmigan were flying about the rocks higher up, and below the sparrows were responding in song to the spring sun.

I had to press on and took a course downward toward the basin, finding it extremely difficult to descend over the steep ground, made very slippery by the melting of much snow on the slopes, and my moccasins affording no foothold whatever. Lying on my side I worked slowly along until I came to a long strip of snow stretching downward in such a way that in order to reach the basin I was obliged to cross it. It extended down a thousand feet, to precipices rising from the stream which there left the foot of the basin. I had crept out over the snow only a few feet when suddenly it gave way, carrying me with it about five feet, before I succeeded in stopping myself, but I was in a position where it seemed doubtful if I could move either up or down, and the danger was extreme. Obliged to act, I jammed the butt of my rifle into the ground and took a step or two, then the snow again gave way, and I went with it. Quickly dropping the rifle, turning on my stomach, and stretching out my arms to try to cling to the ground, I went on constantly slipping with increasing momentum and feeling that I was going to eternity. I began to revolve and to descend diagonally, when suddenly, at a depression in the slope, I stopped myself with feet and hands at the edge of the snow bank. The rifle, having followed me downward, slipped under me as I stopped. The entire surface of my hands was badly torn and bleeding, the front sight of the rifle was broken off, and the barrel was filled with snow. Taking off the slippery moccasins, I found it much easier to proceed. Then I cleaned the rifle with the string cleaner always carried in the butt, and slowly descended to a point not so steep, where, after putting on my moccasins, I sat on a rock to look over the basin.

Suddenly, to my intense surprise and satisfaction, I saw a large bear just emerging from the woods across the entrance to the foot of the basin. It at once began to feed on the grass growing on a little knoll. It would pick out the grass, and every few moments throw up its head and toss it about, sniffing. Not once did it look about, but seemed to depend wholly on its power of scent to detect the approach of danger. I was a quarter of a mile from the bear, well above it, and the wind was exactly right for an approach in a straight line. I soon began to move down the incline, watching carefully as I did so; stooping low as the bear faced me, and advancing whenever its head turned in any other direction. Not once did it look or listen, and I was safe from its scenting me. I had studied the ground; and having reached the steep hillside traversing the foot of the basin I worked across it to within two hundred yards of the bear, which was still feeding about the little knoll. I had reached a point where the slope was so steep that I could not advance with safety, yet the salmon-berry bush and alders which covered the knoll made it difficult to get a shot here. Seating myself, however, I watched my chance to fire. Though I tried to aim behind the foreshoulder, on account of the broken sight it was somewhat a matter of guesswork, but I heard the bullet strike and saw the bear jump; it ran a few feet upward and stopped a moment in bewilderment. When I fired again and evidently missed, it quickly turned with a spring and came running at full speed directly toward me. I was surprised to see how rapidly it covered the ground on a steep slope.

My footing was not secure, and in a sitting position I could not seem to cover the running bear with the rifle; hence as it came to within a hundred yards of me, I half rose; then it saw me and turned, rushing down hill. Had I been that hundred yards nearer and without experience, I could, conscientiously perhaps, have written a fine story about a vicious, charging bear. It crossed the stream with a splash, and stopped for a moment *to look up at the spot where it had been feeding.* This seems to show that, even after seeing me, the bear thought the shot had come from the opposite direction. Somewhat similar to this, I believe, are most of the reported cases of the "charging" of bears; some true, but misunderstood. As it paused, I fired, and when the bullet struck it the bear gave a great spring upward and

ran for the timber. As I fired again it almost turned
a somersault, but kept on and soon entered the woods
as my fifth shot missed. Though an indifferent shot,
I could certainly have killed this bear before it reached
the woods had not my rifle-sight been broken off.

Crossing the stream, I found a very bloody trail,
which indicated that one of the bullets at least had
touched a lung. I followed rapidly through the woods
on the trail which led down a steep hill to another
creek. The bear had descended with long jumps, and
wherever its forefeet had touched the ground, there
was a quantity of blood, evidently thrown from its
mouth and nose. Just before reaching the creek, it
had leaped down a ledge ten feet high. The trail
led up another steep hill, and down again to another
creek, and then upward until it reached ground covered with snow. It was now six o'clock. Higher and
higher it went, up to the deep snow, where each step
had sunk in a foot or more. Now I was near timber
line. The snow was so soft and deep, the slope so
steep, that I could scarcely follow the trail, but kept
on as it began to wind up the mountain-side. Finally,
rounding an elevation on the slope higher up above
timber, I saw the well-defined bloody trail leading up
the mountain-side in the distance, and just under the
crest of the range, the bear itself, slowly struggling,
step by step, upward. I thought at first it would not
reach the top, that it would fall and roll at any moment, and from time to time it did stop, apparently
staggering, but only again to toil on.

In my moccasins it was impossible to follow up the

steep slope at that late hour, and suicidal to be caught in the dark on top of that rough, bleak, snowy mountain; reluctantly, therefore, I sat and watched the bear through my field-glasses. It would lie down a moment, then rise staggering, take a few steps, and rest again, until it finally reached the crest, along which it began to walk slowly, its form clearly visible on the sky-line, where it still kept looking about for danger. It was a magnificent sight, that bear displaying its huge dark bulk on the sky-line of that mountain-girdled valley, while it walked along the crest to the top of the highest, roughest peak, slowly pacing back and forth, looking for a place to lie down. As the twilight deepened, it descended a few feet to the side of the peak facing the basin and lay down on the verge of a precipice falling into what appeared to be a great pit surrounded by perpendicular cliffs. The bear kept changing its position, apparently in distress, and every few moments would struggle to its feet and look about, as if an enemy were approaching. Finally it stretched out on its side and moved a little, as if it were panting. I knew it would die, and as darkness began to come on, had to leave, smarting under keen disappointment. I was sure that it would fall into the great pit, which looked inaccessible. I descended, and started through the dark forest toward camp, thinking how all this demonstrated the wild, cautious nature of the bear, and what inaccessible, rough places it seeks when frightened and wounded. On Montague Island bears had never been systematically pursued or hunted, and every experience I have had with them, there and elsewhere, leads me to doubt most of the stories of their aggressive boldness in times past.

With some difficulty I progressed slowly through the darkness, feeling my way with a staff, occasionally listening to hear the echoes of the owl's hooting or feel the charm of the single notes of the varied thrushes, sweetly sounding in the stillness of the woods. My hands were in bad condition, and I had been severely punished by the devil's-club, when I reached camp at 11 P. M., to find that my men had put provisions for only one day in the bidarka—an example of the usual lack of foresight in the native. But I slept soundly in the wretched little barrábara, my hope still high of getting that bear the next day.

May 8.—I breakfasted before daylight and put a new front sight on my rifle as the dawn ushered in a perfect day, calm, sunny, and mild. Sending my natives back to the bay for provisions, I started for the basin. Reaching the foot and climbing to timber line, I looked through my glasses. I could not see the bear where it had been the evening before, but the bloody slide over the snow below indicated plainly what had happened. I was now wearing hobnail shoes, and at once began the ascent. There was some danger from the numerous snow-slides occurring at intervals, and the last two hundred feet were doubtful, but finally climbing to the crest and walking along it, I reached the point, looked over with eagerness, and this is what I beheld: a great circular pit about three hundred feet across, completely surrounded by perpendicular cliffs and precipices, falling two hundred or three

Route along face of mountain.   May 7.

o Where I fell; snow concealed behind a ledge.
✛ Spot where bear was feeding.
- - - - Course of bear after the first shots.

Head of basin.   May 8.
✛ Point where I first saw bear and cub.

hundred feet to the bottom. There, partly stretched
on its side, was my bear lying dead, while two male
bald eagles were tearing out and eating its entrails.
Through my glasses it appeared about six feet long,
whitish on the back and sides. Its legs were dark, and
a narrow blackish tinge extended from its head along
the spine to the tail. I circled the pit, but could find
no possible path of descent. Only the impressive
beauty of snow, mountains, green woods, and vast
expanse of sea softened my deep disappointment when
I was forced to leave and retrace my steps down the
mountain-side to a point where I could look well over
the basin and the bare slopes about.

At exactly 2 P. M., high up near the mountain crest,
near the head of the basin, a mile distant, I saw through
my glasses a bear descending over the snow, the trail
behind showing that it had just come over the mountain-top, probably having left its winter cave shortly
before. Soon I saw a cub running about with it.

It was not possible to attempt a stalk high up in
the snow, on the steep slopes. Quickly descending, I
reached the snow field at the head of the basin and
climbed to a point where I could watch her. The old
bear did not descend, but was pottering about, digging in the snow to reach grass or mice, while she fed
over a few bare rocky spaces that were exposed. At
short intervals she kept throwing up her head, swinging it back and forth to sniff the air, but not once did
she *look* about for danger. She continued to feed
over a small area for some time without descending,
and then started circling the mountain-side, high up,

just under the cliffs and precipices of the crest. I noticed that she travelled ahead, while the cub followed, lagging somewhat behind, but always stepping in the mother's tracks, so that the trail, except when the cub occasionally deviated for a short distance in shallow snow, appeared as one continuous track. I noticed also that the cub was limping. At first the old bear travelled only short distances, still digging and feeding while the cub played about, now lying down, now running, now watching its mother dig.

I yielded to the fascinating pastime of watching them through my glasses, until the old bear began to travel without stopping, descending slightly; then I thought that by crossing the basin and reaching a clump of spruces fairly high on the slope, I might anticipate them and get a shot. Descending, I crossed the narrow gorge, choked with ice and snow and full of deep cracks through which I could hear the creek rushing twenty or thirty feet below; I reached the spruces, and had a favorable wind for their approach. I soon caught a glimpse of them, now higher up, travelling ahead, but they quickly disappeared around a swell in the ridge and did not come in sight for some time. When they did, they were just under the crest and moving fast. My hopes sank as I saw them continue to go forward and completely circle the basin without descending below the snow. At last they reached some jutting cliffs and stopped to feed about the rocks, climbing over and among them like mountain sheep. I would never have believed that any large animal, except a sheep or a goat, could appear so much at home in such a place. High on the cliffs was a depression extending into a space where some stunted spruces grew, and in this wild, lofty spot, at 8 P. M., the old bear laid herself down to sleep, and the cub soon joined her. I was greatly puzzled to find this bear so cautious and timid, as her every action indicated, and could not understand why she had not descended to the grassy pastures of the mountain slopes below the snow. But as twilight was deepening I had to restrain my eagerness for a closer acquaintance, and started back, intending soon to visit this basin again. As I walked, a beautiful white rock ptarmigan strutted before me on the snow, erecting its red combs, and allowing me to approach within ten feet before it flew and alighted only a few yards below.

When I entered the woods it was clear above and absolutely still, yet not quite dark enough to obscure the ground. The air was soft and balmy, and as I passed gorges, water-falls, and spots of strange beauty, the towering white mountains were indistinctly visible through the trees. Many a time, as I crossed the open glades, when I could enjoy a more unobstructed view of the encircling mountain crests, I paused to listen to the sweet, single, drawn-out notes of the varied thrushes, then sounding from the tree tops, beginning low, swelling to full vibrant tones, and at last melting away in the mysterious darkness of the forest—a mystic cradle song, lulling the dim woods to sleep. It was long after dark when I reached camp, to find the natives returned with the provisions and the report that they had seen two bears feeding high on a spur near the coast, about two miles below camp. Old Mark and two native boys, having left the schooner at the north end of the island, had also come to visit us.

May 9.—They passed the night in the little barrá-bara, while I slept, eagerly waiting for the next day's hunt. The stars were twinkling in a clear sky when I breakfasted, but there was a light breeze from the northeast—a bad sign. Old Mark and the boys were leaving, so as to get back to Nuchek before the wind increased. I started up the beach with Misha, who was to show me the mountain where he had seen the bears feeding. We had gone only a short distance when a shout was heard, and we knew at once that Mark was calling us and was in sight of bears. Quickly we returned, the bidarka was launched, and soon we were gliding toward Mark's bidarka, which was well out from the shore, nearly a mile up the coast. When we reached it he explained that he had seen two bears, which had just disappeared in a hollow below the crest of the spur. I was quickly put ashore, and having selected, from the boat, a line of ascent and approach, returned half a mile to circle upward on the spur and get the wind in my favor. The bears were seen on a high ridge, grassy on and near the top, where clear spaces alternated with patches of snow. The ridge extended parallel with the coast, connecting with a mountain, higher and more massive, just beyond. As I entered the woods to cross over and ascend the lower end of the ridge, clouds began to gather. At last I reached the top, to find it at this end covered with stunted spruce, alders, and dense salmon-berry brush,

through which I had to force my way, and as I circled
to the other side and began to move in the direction
of the bears, progress was slow.

It soon became like a typical stalk for mountain
sheep, except that I was uncertain just where the bears
were. The view of the basin on the left, as I caught
glimpses of it between the mists continually drifting
by in the wind, was particularly beautiful. It was
very narrow, the surface was broken and rugged, and
the slopes of the mountains seemed to wall it in, so
that it appeared very deep. A dense fog soon settled
down, the wind freshened, and I kept on in great
uncertainty, but coming nearer to the spot where the
bears had been seen, which had been indicated as a
hundred yards below the top. The fog kept lifting and
falling, a circumstance which only added to my caution. As I approached what I thought was the spot,
I found the crest clear, its rolling, grassy surface covered with bear tracks, and all about were fresh diggings where the animals had been pawing the earth for
mice. Now I was keenly alert, knowing that in the
fog I might at any moment come close upon the bears.
I was well back on the crest, the wind was entirely in
my favor, and the ground was so soft that my shoes
made no noise.

It was with strange sensations that I advanced
through that mysterious fog, with eyes and ears
strained to detect any sign of the bears which at any
moment might appear before me. Finally, crossing
the top, I looked over, believing that I was nearly opposite the point where the bears had been last seen.

The fog had suddenly cleared, the blue sky appeared with a shining sun. I was not quite far enough; and again dropping back behind the crest, I kept on for three hundred yards and cautiously advanced to look over. There I saw, a hundred yards below, the bulky body of a whitish bear stretched out sound asleep, its head curled under its chest, its back toward me. It was lying on the edge of a dense patch of alders in a hollow depression of the slope, which just beyond was very steep and thickly covered with salmon-berry and alders—a well-chosen spot for concealment and rest. The natives had told me that when two bears were together the dark one was always a male, the light one a female, and both Mark and Misha had reported that one of these bears was dark. I could see only the light one, but knew that the other was lying near, in the alders.

With rifle cocked and ready, slowly and noiselessly I began moving down the slope, my eyes fastened on the sleeping bear. Imagine the fascination of such moments—high up on that mountain-side, facing the sea below boiling with white-caps and sounding with the distant roar of the breakers! Step by step I approached. Soon I stooped low and crept to within almost a hundred feet, when I caught sight of a blackish object in the alders, a few feet to the right of the sleeping bear, and knew it to be the other lying concealed. What wild, shy, timid animals! Little by little I crept on, coming nearer and nearer, until there were only seventy-five feet between us, when suddenly I saw the head of the dark bear in the alders rise.

Almost simultaneously I sat down, with rifle pointed. Its head was toward me, and, having seen me as it half rose in surprise, I fired at its heart. Up it came with a great spring, and I fired again at the same spot. It began to run, and with a few jumps disappeared over the slope as I fired a third shot at its hind-quarters.

At the first shot the other bear had sprung to its feet, and was jumping a few feet in one direction, a few feet in another, in great excitement and alarm, thoroughly perplexed, and completely uncertain as to what was happening until, when the dark bear ran, it began to follow. As it ran, I fired at the side toward me; it swerved to the right, and again I fired as it disappeared down the slope. Quickly putting in a fresh clip of cartridges and running forward, I saw the dark bear lying dead, twenty feet below in the thick brush. Without stopping, I turned to the right, and found a bloody trail leading to a thicket of low, dense spruces fifty feet down the slope in the thick salmon-berry brush. There I heard the light bear thrashing about, but could not see it. Cocking my rifle and forcing my way into the spruces, I came to within ten feet of it —thoroughly excited by such close proximity to a wounded bear in dense brush—before I heard it run out on the other side and descend. Following as fast as I could down the steep salmon-berry slopes, I soon saw it indistinctly through the brush fifty yards below. I fired twice, but it kept on. I forced my way downward on the bloody trail, knowing the bear was hard hit. Coming to a landslide, I found the bear had jumped onto it and had run or slid a hundred yards to the thick

brush below. The landslide was too steep for me to keep
my footing, and crossing above, I descended parallel
with it over ground so steep that I was obliged to let
myself slowly down by holding on to the alders. Having descended two hundred yards, I noticed the salmon-
berry bushes shaking, and going a little farther, saw the
bear, badly wounded, a hundred yards below. Finally,
succeeding in finding a clear space between myself
and the bear, I fired at the centre of its body.
It dropped and remained motionless. I reached it
quickly and found it lying on its stomach, caught in
the alders, one hind foot completely wedged in. It
did not stir, though it was breathing heavily. It died
without a struggle, and proved to be a male. The first
shot had been fired at eleven-thirty, and it was now
twelve.

The clouds and mists had again gathered, and since it
was then too dark to photograph, without touching it I
started for camp, reaching there at two-thirty. It was
impossible to convince the natives that the two bears
were dead, but after taking a bite of bread and a cup
of tea I started back with them, trying to rouse them
from their reluctance and indifference. Their doubts,
however, were replaced by great excitement when we
reached the light bear, and this became enthusiasm
when, after passing on, we arrived at the spot where
the other lay.

After cutting away the brush, I had tried to photograph the light bear, but the sky was heavily overcast
and a slight rain was falling. The dark bear also
proved to be a male. It was in fair pelage up to the

"Lying on its stomach, caught in the alders." May 9.

"I saw the dark bear lying dead, twenty feet below in the thick brush." May 9.

neck, where the hair had begun to wear off. After photographing it as it fell, we pulled it up to a more level place at the edge of the depression, where I photographed it again, and carefully measured it, after which we skinned it. While we were thus occupied, two ravens, evidently greatly excited, kept darting down at us again and again. Taking the skin and skull, we descended to the other bear, and after taking off its skin, also cut off a quantity of meat, which I put in my rücksack together with the two skulls. Each man took a skin, and we reached camp at 10 P. M. The dark bear had received two bullets through the heart, both of which passed entirely out on the other side, and one in the hind-quarters, which broke one leg and penetrated well into the interior of the body. Its length was five feet six and one-half inches, height at foreshoulder four feet. All five bullets had entered the second bear. The first struck the neck, severing the jugular, the second broke a foreleg, two struck the hind-quarters, while the last hit the centre of the body. The slope was so steep and the brush so thick that even with the assistance of two men I found it impossible to measure it accurately. Neither bear had much fat, and the pelage on both was about the same. They were young bears, evidently twins, and had not separated since leaving the mother four or five years before. The stomachs of both contained nothing but grass and *Microtus* mice; the first contained five, the second four. The heads of all the mice were crushed, but the bodies were unmutilated.

Between the time of going up the beach and return-

ing later we saw two places where land-otters had passed
to the water to feed. These are exceedingly abundant on the island, as shown by their numerous tracks
on the beach and slides on the benches of the creeks.
Oyster-catchers were common on the shore, and a great
number of crows were feeding about the kelp at low
tide, while cormorants were perched in picturesque
attitudes on nearly every high rock and reef. Up to
that day, since I had only seen the bald eagles sitting
on the trees near the shore, or flying low, I had begun
to feel a little ashamed of our national emblem; but
my pride was partially restored when, after the fog
cleared, I saw them sailing against the sun, resplendent
with white head and tail, soaring high over the mountain tops, circling about the snowy crests, and floating
across the valleys.

There I was, sitting by the fire with two fine bear-
skins and skulls before me! On the two previous days
I had killed one bear and seen another with a cub.
Complete was my exultation and bright were my
hopes for the days to come. Before sleeping I prepared some shrews and mice that had been taken in
the traps.

May 10.—We spent the whole of the next day, which
was fairly clear, fleshing, preparing, and salting the
skins. It required most of the day to flesh them thoroughly, though my men were constantly at work and
very expert, as are all the natives of this region. Late
in the afternoon I took my rifle and walked two miles
down the beach, but, seeing no bear tracks, returned.
The east beach, for the whole length of the island, is

"We pulled it to a more level place."   May 9.

very rough and rocky and strewn with vast quantities
of driftwood of every kind and description. This
means abundance of good fuel for the camp-fire, planks
for shelter, and suitable lumber for native paddles or
any other purpose. Just below our camp the rocks
and reefs jut far out in the water; here I sat for a while
on the highest rock, yielding myself to the fascination
of the scene. The wind was blowing strongly, the tide
coming in, the water breaking, foaming, and dashing
on the rocks with a roar, throwing up clouds of spray;
screaming gulls were circling about and flocks of
cormorants were flying low up and down the coast.
Bald eagles were flying back and forth; now and then
a flock of sandpipers appeared, to vanish behind the
point, while black oyster-catchers whistled as they
skipped about the rocks in search of food.

May 11.—The rain was falling as I slept, and in the
morning a northeast storm had descended, a gale was
blowing, the sea booming, and torrents of rain were
beating down. I sat in the barrábara all day. There
were two cheerful sounds: a fox-sparrow kept constantly singing in the thick spruces near by, and a tiny
winter wren continued to trill its exquisite song from
the gloomy woods.

Misha's occupation interested me. He had brought
the entrails of both bears to prepare for a *kamlayka.*
He had kept them soaked in water all the day before,
and now took a teaspoon and with it carefully scraped
the fat from them as he passed them over a log—an
operation requiring time and patience when repeated
so frequently as he found necessary—until they were

perfectly clean. Then he tied one end with a string and, placing the other in his mouth, blew into it until the entire length of the gut was well inflated—from two to three inches in diameter—after which he tied the other end and coiled it, thus distended, on a peg near the fire. It required less than twenty-four hours to dry thoroughly. Before the inflating process I measured the length of each. That of the dark bear was fifty-four feet and seven inches long, that of the light one fifty-one feet and five inches. Misha said that later, after the bears have fed more, the gut becomes much larger in diameter. When dry and the air is out they can be folded in a small ball, and are thus brought to the women, who cut them in suitable strips and sew them together to form a *kamlayka*. They prize such a *kamlayka* more than anything else that they possess.

May 12.—The following day the storm continued, and I patiently endured it. During this storm, since all the woods and mountains were enveloped in dense fog, it was useless to attempt to hunt. Baranof was happy. He was extremely lazy, and to be curled up in the barrábara was just to his taste; he was even most reluctant to do a little cooking. No shelter could be much more disagreeable than these small, hastily constructed barrábaras. This one was about seven feet wide and thirteen feet long. The natives take planks, which they hew out of spruce or pick up on the beach, stand them upright to form the side and ends, place two ridge-poles across the top of the end walls, and construct a roof by simply laying planks from the side walls to the ridge-poles, and covering the cracks with additional planks, so that it sheds water without leaking. In the centre of the roof a large hole is left to let out the smoke from the fire inside. The roof is seven feet high at the middle, and slopes to the sides, which are about two feet in height. The planks of the walls are seldom tight, but leave spaces from a quarter of an inch to an inch in width, through which the air enters on all sides in a succession of draughts.

The fire is in the centre, where a space of three feet is allowed between rough-plank flooring constructed a foot high and extending to the end walls. In this barrábara the flooring was constructed only on one side, and a space not more than seven feet wide and five long was available for three men to lie side by side. But to sleep one has to draw in his knees, or if he cares to stretch out he must let his feet and legs hang over. After a fire is made the interior at.once becomes filled with smoke, and as this does not all escape through the hole at the top, it remains suspended within three feet of the ground, so that one cannot stand up or even raise his head above that height without choking. In rainy weather the interior becomes very damp and cold. In addition to my misery at staying inside, Misha was suffering from consumption in an advanced stage, and while he slept or lay by me, coughed all through the day and night. Several times I went out to walk in the foggy, drizzling woods, and after each excursion really enjoyed the task of drying my clothes. But the day passed, and the next morning it looked like clearing.

After several years hunting American big game, this

is the only case where I have felt it necessary to tax
the credulity even of my friends. Nevertheless, that
next evening I wrote *facts* in my journal with the utmost care, and the following is a literal transcription:

"*Saturday, May* 13.—To-day I had the most remarkable experience of my life. It cleared about nine-
thirty, so I was off, intending to go three miles down
the beach and up a creek, to a basin well back in the
mountains. A great number of crows, hundreds, are
always feeding about the rocks at low water, and several pairs of black oyster-catchers were evidently preparing to breed. I went up the creek, hearing water-
ouzels on the way, and finally emerged from a deep
canyon, through which the water rushed, leaping down
here and there in cascades, and in some places under
ice and snow. Just before reaching the foot of the
basin, I turned up the south ridge, keeping in the woods
in order to get high on the mountain slopes, and keep
my wind above any bears that might be feeding below,
as it was blowing strong up the basin. I reached the
top of the ridge at 1 p. m. The other side sloped down
to a creek flowing from another basin, and at that point
led abruptly up to the great mountain on the south
side of the basin I was to enter. Coming out of the
timber, I was at the foot of a conical hill two hundred
feet high and very steep; the top was covered with thick,
stunted, impenetrable spruce which extended ten feet
down the slope and continued around it through a
depression to more open timber beyond, where the
hill joined the main mountain. I climbed this hill
diagonally, looking on fine, red-tipped grass for bear

tracks, but saw none. On reaching the spruces I passed around the edge of the trees, holding on to the branches for assistance in walking around the incline.

"I went high up and tramped along the mountain-side. The basin was beautiful, with high, rough mountains encircling it; the air was filled with the rumble and roar of numerous snow slides; starting high up, near the crests of the surrounding mountains, and appearing like immense cataracts, the snow dashed over cliffs and fell through ravines, until it slid in great masses over the smoother ground below, piling up in huge mounds as it stopped. I noticed many marmots about, some sitting up, some running about the snow near the mountain-tops. At different points high up in the snow bear tracks were visible. Reaching a good lookout, I waited until five, watching carefully on all sides, but nothing appeared.

"Then I retraced my steps along the slope and reached the conical hill around which I had passed earlier in the day. I was circling near the top, holding on to the spruce branches with my right hand, while the butt of my rifle, with the barrel pointing behind me, was resting over my left elbow. I had proceeded in this way a few steps when suddenly I saw, about eight feet away, on the curving border of the spruces, running directly at me, what appeared to be a huge bear. I had just time to push forward the butt of my rifle and yell, when the bear collided with me, knocking me down. It seemed to turn slightly to the left as I pushed my rifle into it, and I clearly recall its shoulder striking my left hip, its head striking just above my left knee, while its claws struck my shin so that it is now black and blue. I had the sensation of one about to be mauled and mutilated. As I fell to the right, my rifle dropped, and in my confusion I grabbed with my left hand the animal's fur, and I remember having a quick, foolish thought of the small knife in my pocket.

"The bear was, I believe, more surprised than I. I felt its fur slip through my hand as it quickly turned to its right and, swinging about, ran back over the hill without any attempt to bite or strike me. Rising, as the bear wheeled, I picked up my rifle and shot as the animal was disappearing. The bullet struck it, evidently high in the back. Immediately I took up its trail, followed it down into the woods and on the flats for over an hour, and at last lost the impressions on hard ground. Its tracks showed that it had kept running for more than a mile, and then settled down to a walk on the timbered ridges, continuing to a flat country below. For the first mile I noticed, at intervals, considerable blood on the leaves of brush and trunks of trees, about three feet up from the ground, but afterward saw no more.

"Who will believe this remarkable incident? Certainly if another had related it to me, I might have thought it some mistake owing to excitement.

"Twice I have had the good-luck to see the action of a bear when it crossed, unexpectedly, the fresh trail of a man—once in Mexico, and again last summer, on the MacMillan River, when a bear crossed Selous's trail. In both cases the bear jumped in great fright and ran at full speed. In this case, when the bear met me, I

"The basin was beautiful with the high, rough mountains encircling it."   May 13.

was approaching the top of the hill by the simplest,
in fact the only easy, route, along the edge of the thick
spruces.   My trail, made earlier in the afternoon, came
over the hill from the north side.   I found that the
bear had ascended from a direction diagonally opposite,
and had reached my trail near the top just as I was
approaching; running, it kept its course in the same
direction, and took the natural route around the hill,
close to the spruces, in order to enter the woods farther
on, where they were not so thick, or to make for the
mountain.   At this exact moment I happened along,
but, concealed by the curve of the spruces, and with
the wind blowing from the bear to me, it did not sus-
pect my presence until I yelled at the moment of collision.   The fact that it did not maul me, and ran so
quickly, is positive proof of its having been completely
surprised.   Still, I do not care to repeat the sensations
I experienced at that moment.   Here is another case
where many would have reported a vicious charge.   I
regret having been in such haste to take up the trail
that I neglected to photograph the spot.

"After losing the trail, I climbed a ridge and ascended
the mountain-side of another basin, even more beautiful than the first, and at that hour everything was
softened and mellowed in the light of the declining sun;
the blend of the bare slopes and snow seemed to glow,
the deep sky-coloring merged into the stern outline
of the jagged mountain crests.   I looked about and
watched, but as no bear tracks were visible on the snow
and nothing appeared, I returned three miles to the
beach, where I made a cup of tea, and reached camp

at 11 P. M. The days are longer; it was delightful to walk in the twilight and dusk along the rock-bound shore, with the waves breaking gently over the reefs and falling softly on the beach. Bald eagles were soaring about, gulls were skimming the waves, and everywhere cormorants were perched on the rocks, about to sleep. Even the oyster-catchers were in a sitting posture and allowed me to approach quite close. Nature was in her gentlest mood.

"My men have not put out the bear-skins, but have allowed them to remain folded all day in the barrá-bara. Since they cannot be trusted to do what I tell them, I cannot start to-morrow until I see it done."

May 14.—It required more than an hour after day-light to cut stakes, construct frames, and hang the bear-skins. Immediately after this was done I started over the mountains to hunt the extreme north basin on the coast—the only one in that direction which I had not examined. It was a pleasant day, and I climbed the same mountain on which I had stalked the bears. Approaching the carcass of the first one, I saw a ruddy-horned (?) owl sitting near by on a knoll, and coming nearer was surprised to see about forty bald eagles, some sitting about, gorged, others circling near, and still others picking away the flesh. Little remained but the skeleton. Transformed into carrion-feeders, the eagles acted exactly like vultures, and those at the carcass allowed me to approach within fifty feet before they reluctantly rose and scattered, soaring all about the mountains.

I kept ascending, went across the snow-fields to the

peak, and descended to a point on the other side, whence I could watch and examine the basin beyond. Several marmots were running on the snow about the very peak; along the lower crest not far from where I had killed the bears I photographed a ptarmigan sitting on the edge of a vast precipice overlooking the sea below. It was alone, and allowed me to approach fairly close. I watched the basin until five, and did not see even the tracks of a bear; hence descended directly to the beach and reached camp at 9 P. M. Daylight was still lingering, for twilight settled later each night. While walking down the beach I saw a bald eagle's nest in one of the large spruces near, and by the way the birds acted it was clear that young ones were in it. My men, always blissfully content with sitting in camp smoking the tobacco I had brought for them, as well as drinking tea every hour in the day and gorging themselves with the fishy bear meat, reported seeing a bear on the beach, close to camp. Though it had rained a little in the morning I could see no tracks, and knew they were only revealing to me their imaginings.

May 15.—I went up to the basin behind camp, in the hope that the bear and cub had settled there to feed regularly. Though a great deal of snow had melted, I noticed that the tracks of the bear I had wounded were still so plain from a distance that the trail looked fresh. On the snow above I saw also the trail of the bear and cub continuing high under the crest to the lower end; there it passed over the top into the next basin, beneath the spot where I had the collision with the bear. They had not loitered there. Having watched until seven without seeing anything, I returned, knowing that we must move south to explore new basins. A few days before, I had noticed in the heavy spruce-trees, on a ridge, a small hummock about two feet high, on and about which were strewn numerous feathers, heads, and bones of jays and ptarmigans, some probably a year old, others quite fresh. As I passed the place again that day, I saw the feathers and bones of a ptarmigan not twenty-four hours old. It is interesting thus to observe how an owl—probably the ruddy-horned—will bring its captured prey to the same spot again and again to feed upon it. Although owls were fairly common, I did not see a hawk on Montague Island all the time I was there.

May 16.—The next morning was clear, but there was too much surf to launch the bidarka. At one o'clock, however, we made the attempt, and succeeded. As we went a few miles down the coast, the wind died out, leaving a swell so heavy that we could not land, and had to turn back, thus losing a day. On reaching our old camp, where the beach was fairly smooth, Misha was afraid to attempt a landing, and both my companions insisted on returning to Zaïkof Bay, where the water was always smooth. It was only by tact, and by touching their pride as bidarka men, that I succeeded in inducing them to make the attempt; the landing was accomplished without any bad result other than that of filling the bidarka half full of water and thoroughly wetting all our stuff on the inside. There were few days without a swell, and this is one of the great difficulties of hunting on Montague Island. One must keep moving down the coast to hunt new basins, and the bidarka is the only means of transportation.

Since those made by the Nuchek natives are so small, I was wedged in and had to be helped out. If the breakers are at all heavy, landing is dangerous, and the boat is very likely to be destroyed. The natives as they paddle always kneel in the port-holes, and when landing in the breakers they can quickly spring out and pull the bidarka up on the beach. If this is not done quickly, the next wave rolling in is quite apt to turn it and break it. Thus, my being unable to get out always necessitated landing where there was little swell, and in a smooth place. Very few, if any, white men can kneel in the bidarka after the manner of the natives, which is much more difficult and tiresome than the common sitting attitude of the Turk or Japanese.

As we returned too late in the afternoon to hunt, I attended to the bear-skins and put them out in the sun. Later we saw the little sloop of the prospectors sailing north, far out from the shore, returning at that hour necessarily to Zaïkof Bay.

CHAPTER VII

HUNTING THE BIG BEAR (Concluded)

May 17.—Since there was not so much swell the next day, which was bright and clear, we started early, and at noon arrived at the point selected, ten miles down the coast. Here the beach was rough, and we could not land in the breakers. The natives wanted to turn back, but I persuaded them to keep on, and three miles farther down we, with some difficulty, made a landing at the mouth of a small creek where there was a little barrábara. After taking a cup of tea, I soon started, climbed a high mountain to command the basin, and then waited and watched, enchanted by the new scenery. The landscape here was beautiful and very rugged. Snow had filled in whole valleys, and over precipices and through gorges dashed many a cascade, high above the level of the sea.

The day was perfectly still and calm. While I scanned the basin with my field-glasses, the sparrows all about were fairly bursting with song; the ptarmigan, flying from rock to rock above, kept sounding their croaking chatter, and from the woods far below I could distinctly hear the pleasing song of the varied thrush.

I could see only a few tracks on the snow, and the ground was so rough, the mountain slopes so broken, that even if a bear were seen it was doubtful if a successful stalk could be made. I therefore started back, feeling that to return to this group of basins would be a waste of valuable time, and intending the next day to try one we had passed farther up the shore.

That night we slept under the stars on the beach. It was clear, calm, and peaceful. The steady roar of the surf, the soft air, the ocean so close to me, induced a feeling of delicious contentment, which, by its very contrast with the discomfort of my many nights in the disagreeable barrábara, kept me awake for a long time.

May 18.—We were aroused early in the morning by a hard rain which obliged us to put everything in the little excuse for a hut, barely large enough for three of us to squeeze into, and leaking badly.

About ten the rain stopped, though showers and mists, alternating with sunny skies, continued all through the day, and a strong wind blew from the east. I went up the beach to hunt a large basin about two miles above, while my men started in the bidarka to land and make a camp at the point we had failed to reach the day before, about three miles beyond the creek of the basin. Before long I came upon some bear tracks on the beach, which continued for about fifty yards, to where the bear had again entered the woods. This was the first bear track I had seen on the beach. Reaching the mouth of the creek coming from the basin, I took out my field-glasses and examined the side of a high mountain fairly overhanging the sea—the broad, steep face of a spur separating this basin from the next. High up, just under the snow, feeding about the grassy slope, I saw a bear, and my glasses soon revealed a cub playing about it. A strong wind was blowing directly up the basin; there remained, therefore, only one method for successful approach— to circle on the steep slope and pass between some jutting cliffs. But it would require time to make the climb, and should the bear, in the interval, move two hundred yards west along the slope, the stalk would be a failure because of the wind and exposure. I decided, therefore, to wait and watch for a more favorable opportunity. Sure enough, the bear and the cub kept on feeding slowly in the direction I had feared, and I congratulated myself on not having made the attempt.

It was a quarter past eleven when I first saw the bear, and for nearly two hours I waited, watching it from the beach. The old bear kept gradually moving around the slope, up toward the basin, feeding all the time. It occurred to me that perhaps female bears with cubs had to feed longer than others to keep up the milk supply. Finally, in order to hold them in sight, I had to go some distance through the woods and climb a ridge to the foot of the clear slope above timber line. While doing this I noticed a fairly well-beaten bear trail parallel with the coast, just inside the woods. Arriving at the foot of the slope, I saw the old bear feeding opposite, high up, just under the snow line, not a quarter of a mile above me, and noticed for the first time that the *cub was limping*. It was the identical bear and cub I had seen May 8, and they had kept travelling daily to this point, circling every basin, always high up, on or just below the snow, crossing the successive mountain tops, as I learned later by observing their trail in the remaining basins. Again

I failed to understand their extreme caution. It was
with eagerness that I watched the bear, now so near,
and how I longed to come within shot!

She kept picking up grass, and every little while
would stop to dig out a mouse, when the cub would
always run up to her, smell about, and watch her with
great interest. Every few moments up went the
mother's head, swinging sidewise back and forth, to
sniff the air; and then, for the first time, I saw that she
constantly looked about with extra caution. By the
way she pricked up her ears, she evidently suspected
some sound—that of a bear, I think—from the direction of the basin, for she repeatedly looked at one point.
Twice, as the mother stood still, I saw the cub attempt
to nurse, but it was immediately cuffed away. Finally,
the old bear fed along more rapidly, often crossing
bands of snow which extended well down the slope,
sometimes digging down into the snow for a mouse,
until at last she began to travel without stopping to
feed, always ascending higher. Once she was obliged
to descend slightly in order to pass around the foot of
a cliff, and there, turning upward, she disappeared at
the point where the spur curves to form the basin.
Deciding on what seemed my only chance, I started to
climb diagonally, so as to keep the bear above me and
allow the wind, blowing strong at a right angle to my
line of ascent, to carry my scent below her.

Now I was on a beautiful clear pasture slope, leading
directly to the basin, while all about the surface were
very fresh bear diggings, showing that a bear was regularly feeding there; and it was a matter of great regret

that I was obliged to proceed along it with the wind, and thus perhaps frighten off this other bear that might be feeding or resting beyond. I circled up under the cliffs to the point where the bear was last seen, and found that on the other side the slopes were very high, rocky, and broken with canyons and gorges; nor could I see the bear. I felt that in such a rough country it would be impossible to keep her in sight, and that, as she was travelling, my chances were gone. I went a short distance along the slope to the first gorge, which was filled with snow extending clear up to the snow-line above. *No bear track had crossed it.* I took out my glasses and examined all the snow above—still no bear tracks! Then I knew that she was lying down somewhere directly above me, in the space between the cliffs and the gorge, concealed in one of the clumps of stunted spruce close to the snow-line. I immediately started upward, but found the ascent very difficult. The slope became so steep and precipitous that I could scarcely climb and keep my footing, and had to assist myself by leaning forward and using my left hand, while the rifle remained, uncocked, in my right. I could not risk the noise of using the butt as a staff. The space within which the bear must be lying was not two hundred feet wide, and it became intensely exciting to work upward under such disadvantages, expecting at any instant to see her rise up. Besides, the fact that she had a cub with her made me feel somewhat uncertain of her temper.

Step by step I ascended over the wet grass and moss as noiselessly as possible, stopping every few feet to

"Ptarmigan sitting on the edge of a vast precipice." Hinchinbrook Island
faintly visible. May 14.

"On the other side the slopes were very high, rocky, and broken with canyons
and gorges." May 18.

take breath, until at last I reached a point twenty feet below the snow-line. Suddenly, coming from a bunch of low stunted spruce to my right, on a slope so steep that it seemed almost perpendicular—and not a hundred feet away—I heard a low moaning sound. I could see nothing, but cocked my rifle, and with the greatest caution crept slowly upward a few feet, then carefully lifting my head, I saw the cub pushing its head into the body of its mother. The mother, stretched at length in a slight depression among the spruces, was indistinctly visible, and I saw that her left forefoot was raised. The cub was nursing. It seemed excited with hunger and moved its head about in a mild frenzy, all the time bawling in a low, strange tone.

The ground was so steep and so slippery, because of melting snow, that I was lying on my left side, holding on as I could with my left hand, while my feet could barely get enough support to keep me from slipping, as I held the rifle with the other hand. Quickly I lowered the butt of the rifle to the ground, slowly moved my feet about, and fortunately felt some small stones in such a position as to give me support and allow me to release my left hand so that I could handle the rifle.

I must have made a slight noise, for just at that moment the bear suddenly half rose, her head turned in my direction. I quickly fired at her foreshoulder. With a whoof and a jump she came to her feet, and I fired again. In savage fury, she slapped the point where the bullet had struck, rushed a few feet in the direction away from me, then a few up and a few down, all the time whoofing in pain or fright, and looking for the enemy in the *opposite direction*. The cub remained in the spruces bawling. While the old bear was rushing back and forth, I fired three more times, and at the fifth shot she dropped for a moment in some low spruces. As I rapidly pushed in a fresh clip of cartridges, she began to roll downward, over and over, bounding up and down with the increase of momentum, until five hundred yards below, where the slope was not so steep, she was stopped by thick salmon-berry brush. I knew she was dead before she began to roll.

The cub soon emerged from the spruces and started running to follow its mother. I shot before it had gone three feet. It fell near some other spruces, and, as it began to roll, caught in a small spruce, where it remained almost hanging. My bullet had struck it in the head.

I sat down to rest and to relax the tension under which I had been laboring for those few moments. After glancing at the magnificent mountains and beautiful basins sloping to the soft green timber of the ridges which extended in rolling outlines to the sea, I began to scan more carefully the hills and slopes about, when my eye caught a moving object on the opposite side of the nearest basin. Through my glasses I saw it was a bear of the same size and color as the others I had seen. From the way it sneaked up a ravine, always seeking the thick alders in which to hide at every opportunity, until it passed over a hill and into the woods, it was quite apparent that it was travelling away from danger. Though for hours, at intervals, I kept a watch in that direction, I did not

"She was stopped by thick salmon-berry brush where the slope was not so steep." May 18.

"Caught in a small spruce." May 18.

see it again. It was probably the same bear, then feeding nearer to her, that the old bear had detected as she approached in that direction.

Since the slope was too steep to allow going directly to the cub, I climbed up to the snow and descended to the cub on more favorable ground. It was a beautiful male more than a year old, with thick, luxuriant fur of a rich whitish-brown color and nearly six inches in length. I determined to take off its skin, but, before beginning, seated myself to smoke my pipe and enjoy the landscape. I was burning with the glow produced by that rare glimpse of wild animal life—the very essence of wild nature. I could not resist a strong feeling that I had intruded upon sacred moments in that old bear's life, moments forbidden to the members of the human race by some deep law of nature. Faithfully she had fulfilled her duties. Her last hours had found her still performing them, having hidden so well, on such difficult ground, in a spot high and secluded—taking every precaution to give food to her young. It seemed to me that I had the right to kill her, but not thus to detect her at the time she was giving her breast.

After a while I tried to take some photographs, but the sky unfortunately grew cloudy. The shooting had occurred at three-fifteen in the afternoon. I was obliged carefully to wedge the cub in the spruces, to prevent its falling, as well as to wedge myself in order to work without slipping. No sooner had I begun than a heavy rain came on, and a dense mist settled down, so that I could not see ten feet about me. Thus,

almost suspended in the mysterious mist, I worked to
get the skin off.   The left foreleg of the cub had been
crushed and was completely healed, leaving a large
bunch.   When the skin was separated I noticed a well-
defined circle of tooth-marks about the spot, showing,
beyond doubt, that it had been bitten by the mother,
perhaps in the den, so hard as to crush the leg.   When
the skinning was finished the rain had stopped and it
became clear and calm, though the disturbed surface
of the sea still gave life to the landscape.   The atmosphere was mild, and the lengthening snow shadows
gave contrasting effects as I looked out over the scene
before me.   Ptarmigan—always interesting to watch
as they flew about—were particularly abundant, and
two bald eagles kept soaring above me, circling high
in the heavens and floating over the basins.   The shrill
whistle of the marmot sounded continually on all sides,
above and below, and many a time I saw the animals
scampering about, sitting up or plunging into their
holes, or often taking a position on a rock from which
every few moments their long single whistle would
sound.

No more bears appeared, and at 8 P. M., leaving the
carcass of the cub suspended in a tree, I rolled its shat-
tered skull down the slope.   It continued to fall almost
to the dead bear, which now appeared like a small dark
speck in the salmon-berry bushes below.   I worked
my way down to it, and found a fine old female in excellent pelage, of the same general color, though somewhat browner, than that of the cub.   As it was too late
to take the skin off, rolling her over to keep the blood

from running out and coagulating on the fur, I started for the beach with the skin and skull of the cub in my rücksack. Upon reaching and proceeding along the beach, I saw another track, probably made by the same bear whose track I had seen below on the beach that morning, and which had been walking on the trail just inside of the woods. Bears were evidently beginning to travel more, as before that day I had not seen a track below the basins.

Soon I saw large fires and great clouds of smoke near where I expected to find my men. On reaching the camp I found about twenty natives, including Fred, the chief, old Mark, and his brother Pete, all bound for Wooded Island on a sea-otter hunt. They had stopped when they saw my men on the shore, and, hoping that they might get some meat, were waiting to see if I had killed a bear.

I was greatly annoyed to find that Fred and my boy, Baranof, had been up in the basin behind—a place I was counting on to hunt in the next afternoon—and had gotten in the wind of a bear, at least so they said. But the continual shouting, the great fires, and the clouds of smoke rolling up the basin and through the woods were sufficient to spoil any hunting in the vicinity. The natives were delighted to learn of the carcasses, and all volunteered to go with me the next day to bring back the meat. I had already tried to eat the meat of the other bears killed, but since it was too strongly tainted with a fishy flavor, even after having been so long without fish, to tempt me, I soon desisted, having an abundance of other food.

Now the nights were not entirely dark at any time, and I stretched out in a little loosely constructed plank shelter and fell asleep amid the shouting and laughter of the natives on the beach.

May 19.—The morning was bright, a strong wind was blowing volumes of smoke up the creek, and already Fred and another native—in imitation of what Misha had told them about me—had risen very early and tramped up the basin, completely shattering any lingering hope that I might still find a bear there. They had returned without seeing anything. I took several photographs of the natives, and together we all started down the beach to go to the carcass of my bear. Old Mark told me that a year before he had killed a very large bear in that vicinity, near the beach, and at my suggestion left us to get the skull. We reached the carcass of my bear and, after I had photographed and measured it, began skinning it. Its length was five feet and five inches. It was a very old female. In a short time, with such skilled assistance, the skin was off. When stretched without much tension it measured seven and a half feet long, or two feet longer than the body of the bear; and if it had been taken off fresh it would have stretched much more. I examined its stomach, which was full of grass and contained also seven *Microtus* mice. The mice were quite fresh, the heads only were crushed, the rest of the bodies not mutilated. I had seen the bear digging for mice so many times that it is clear it had not caught one at every attempt.

The natives sent three boys up the mountain to roll

down the cub. The sun had been hot, and since I had not drawn the entrails of either, or opened them, both were badly swollen and the meat was thoroughly tainted, with a strong smell. But this made no difference; the natives cut up the old bear, loaded themselves with every ounce of it, took the cub's carcass without opening it, and we returned to camp. Old Mark was there with the large skull of his male bear, slightly weather-beaten, but perfectly preserved. It was so much larger than my skulls that I was puzzled.

Although the day was perfect, I had to remain in camp and attend to the skins. Fred was about to start for the next basin above, and thus spoil my last chance to hunt fresh ground from that camp, but upon my telling him frankly that I would appreciate it if he did not go, he complied with my request. I have found that with tact one can nearly always handle natives so as to make them obliging. They soon had the meat boiling and were gorging. It seems incredible, but the feast was kept up day and night amid shouting and merriment, and within twenty-four hours not a morsel of the meat remained. The odor of it was sickening.

May 20.—Although the next day was cloudy and rainy, I went up into the next basin above and climbed the mountain. Near that camp, in the basins on all sides, I could see on the snow the trail of the bear and cub, never descending, as it wound about, circling each basin. The rain soon began to fall heavily, the mist descended and enveloped me so that I could not look about. Later, though it kept on raining, the mist cleared away and I watched, but saw nothing, got thoroughly soaked, and late in the evening returned to camp. The following day I intended to move two miles up, make a camp, and try my last hunting.

The natives were still there. They might easily have left and reached their destination that day, but they had been enjoying the feast and were thoroughly indifferent about making any effort. I found that there was not another native in Nuchek, and none would be there until they returned. This was unfortunate, since nobody would be there to help Swanson sail his schooner —he could not do it alone—unless these men returned from their hunt in time to assist him to bring me back to catch the steamer due at Nuchek May 30. Only one steamer a month stopped there. I planned, therefore, to leave in the morning and hunt one basin in the afternoon, then to return the next day to Zaïkof Bay and send Misha and Baranof over to Nuchek in the bidarka to help Swanson back with the schooner. Even then I was taking chances, as bad weather might prevent their crossing in the bidarka.

That day, for the first time, I had seen two mosquitoes. The night was calm and mild. Nature's love song had begun, for more varieties of birds had arrived and sweet music was all about.

May 21.—In the morning my hopes of more hunting were dashed by the fierce descent of the northeast storm, which continued unabated all day. I had my men continually splitting and bringing in wood, and kept the bear-skins stretched under the shelter before a fire, and attended to them the whole day. I was greatly in-

terested when Fred, the chief, brought me the bullet
from a thirty-two Winchester rifle, which he had found
lodged in the shoulder of the bear; and old Mark as-
serted that this proved that it was the bear he had
wounded on the beach the preceding fall. This was
probably the reason, in part, of her extreme caution,
and served to explain to me many of her strange actions. My boy, Baranof, who had become practically
inactive, was shirking any possible task, however small,
and was evidently heartily tired of the trip. But I
managed to induce him to perform the few slight tasks
falling to his share.

May 22.—The storm continued all the next day, but
I diligently kept up the fire, so that when the rain
stopped, about eight o'clock, the bear-skins were partially dry. There was little wind during the day, but
the sea-otter hunters continued their merriment and
stayed on, though they could have put on their *kamlaykas* and paddled on to their destiñation. They were
rapidly consuming the provisions that Swanson had
given them, and were only half-way to their hunting-
ground, where they should have been already in order
to take advantage of the favorable condition of the
weather for hunting.

I was interested in observing them during our close
association for the last four days. Half of them were
mere boys, some not over thirteen years of age,
though able to paddle all day in their bidarkas. The
boys were compelled to do all the work of cooking, taking care of the camp, getting wood, building and keeping up the fires. The older men did nothing but eat,

talk, and sleep at intervals all through the day; but two or three were busy at times carving paddles from suitable pieces of driftwood found near by on the beach. It was clear that these natives were most indifferent about the sea-otter hunting, and I felt assured that usually, when travelling to the hunting-grounds, they loitered along the beach, avoiding a reasonable day's paddling until the provisions given them by Swanson began to get low; then they would make a quick dash, hunt only a day or two, and at times return without hunting at all.

The influence of several generations of training by the Russian priests manifested itself in some strange anomalies in their daily habits. Each one had brought a towel and soap, and they never neglected washing their hands every morning. They evidently liked to go through some of the forms of cleanliness, with no appreciation of cleanliness itself, for their hands always became soiled again before eating, and their habits were filthy. One of them knew how to make baking-powder bread. Early one morning I saw him cut open the cub, take out the tainted entrails, and then proceed to wash. Immediately he plunged his hands in the entrails again, and was drawing them when he was called to make bread. Out came his hands, and leaving the cub half full of entrails, he started to knead the dough without washing or even wiping his hands! In the morning each would carefully spread out his blanket and air it—another form, for immediately they would allow oil and dirt of every kind to cover it.

Natives loaded with bear meat.   May 19.

Native sea-otter hunters—Misha at left, Pete and Mark in centre.
May 19.

When two of the older men took a steam bath, they compelled the boys to construct a small enclosed shelter of driftwood, build a fire inside, heat a heap of rocks in it, and produce steam by pouring water over the hot rocks; then one would step inside and sweat for a while, and later sit naked out in the cold air for fifteen minutes or more! They are great talkers, very fond of joking, and, when not sleeping, keep it up so continually that the conversation never lags. The boys sleep at times during the day, but much less than the men. They constantly play, after the manner of little children, and seem perniciously active in all kinds of mischief. A favorite occupation was to whittle out little boats and sail them down the small, narrow creek, using a piece of bark for a sail. They kept this up, one after another, by the hour. Again and again they would construct from driftwood, with much labor, a high, irregular frame, and then, pushing out a prop, cause it to collapse, seemingly having great fun as it tumbled down. At about five o'clock every evening, rain or no rain, they would begin to play what I understood to be a traditional game, without significance other than the fun produced. It is typically a part of "duck-on-the-rock" without the "duck." Two fairly large rocks are placed about thirty-five feet apart; standing by one, the players try to hit the other by pitching at it a smaller rock. Usually some of the older men joined in the game, and it was continued far into the night, with great shouting and even with excitement.

On the whole, I thought the character of these Eskimos like that of most Alaska Indians—lacking in foresight and ambition. They are fond of inactivity, eating, sleeping, playing, social chatter, and are only willing to work under the stress of necessity.

I had to give up hunting, and was then most anxious about getting back in time to catch the steamer.

May 23.—The day broke clear, and I soon left camp to walk several miles up the beach to our first camp, allowing my men to proceed in the bidarka with the bear-skins. The natives discovered a Russian holiday, and, instead of going to the sea-otter ground, remained merry-making where they were. While walking along the beach I saw a bald eagle's nest near by in a large spruce-tree. Both birds kept crying as I went along, and while I stood under the tree the female remained perched on the top, the male sitting in another tree a short distance off. Young were in the nest, and I had noticed before that whenever eagles saw me approaching they would begin to scream in alarm long before I came near the nest.

Soon after 1 P. M. I arrived at the barrábara, where my men had some tea ready. I sent them to Zaïkof Bay with the bear-skins and skulls, instructing them to return the following morning for me and the remaining camp material. Then I started back to the familiar basin, to spend the afternoon among the mountains. The woods were still dripping with moisture, but the day was warm and sunny. When I emerged from timber line, how great the contrast to sixteen days before! Now spring was at hand. The slopes were bright green, the grass long, innumerable wild violets were timidly peeping out everywhere, buttercups and long bands of yellow violets added their gay color to the landscape. All nature seemed laughing with the sun, sweet bird songs sounded on all sides, as the streams, now swollen from melting snow, rushed down the canyons, dashed over precipices in pretty water-falls, or leaped over wooded cliffs in a succession of cascades. I could see the familiar bear tracks and trails in the snow above, now almost obliterated, and I pondered long on the trail of the old female bear, whose skin was now being carried over the water to my shelter tent.

Sadly and regretfully I later returned to camp, realizing that I had done my last wandering among the rugged crests of Montague Island. It had all been most fascinating; the combination of sea, woods, and mountains, in an almost untrodden wilderness, at the season when spring was gently installing itself; and, above all, the delight of watching and stalking the bears, which in May dwell and feed high up near the snowy mountain crests. No animal on the continent is wilder or more wary; none wanders more indifferently in the low woods or along the rivers and shores; and none feeds on the slopes and pastures above timber line more easily, even on the crags and precipices in the midst of ice and sliding snow.

That night I slept close to the water: As I lay on the beach looking up at the faint lights of the stars, it was absolutely clear, the sea in front gently rolled in, breaking on the rocks with a subdued roar. The woods were hushed and peaceful, while behind them the snow-covered mountain crests towered up grim and desolate.

The little winter wren trilled low its warbling song, varied thrushes pealed out their notes in golden key from the tree tops, while near by in the depths of the silent forest sounded the mysterious silver songs of hermit-thrushes.

May 24.—But at six in the morning rain-drops were pattering on my blanket. I hurried everything into the barrábara as the wind and rain increased, and in half an hour there descended the worst northeaster I had yet experienced. The ground from the beach to the barrábara soon became so flooded that I had to wade through a foot of water to bring driftwood to the leaking dwelling, where I split it in the soaking rain, and kept repeating the operation all day to keep the fire going. The sea was magnificent as the mighty breakers rolled in, falling with a crashing roar, almost to the woods. The wind was so strong that the smoke did not escape well, and my eyes became seriously inflamed.

May 25.—By bathing my eyes constantly in cold water, I at last slept, and awoke to find the rain still pouring down, but no wind; and judging by the breakers, there was not so much swell outside. Again I patiently endured a blank day. At six o'clock my men arrived, saying that they had taken great risks because they were worried about me. But I had all the beans, rice, tea, and sugar, and when I saw them eat I knew the true reason of their solicitude.

May 26.—Rain and a heavy fog all the next day, but little wind. Still we accomplished something. We paddled back to the bay, arriving at 1.30, and after eating, the men started for Nuchek to assist Swanson

Baranof and Misha.   May 23.

Mountains around basin behind camp.   May 23.

in bringing his schooner back. By night the rain had ceased, and though the bay was obscured by fog it was calm. After these three gloomy, stormy days I could scarcely realize that I had been wandering high up in the mountains, where the snow glistened all about and the pastures were bright and green, far above the shining sea. My skins were all spread and receiving the warmth of the fire, as, alone, I looked out on the mist and calm. The gulls still screamed; the geese still honked as they flew by; ducks still quacked as they floated lazily about in the water. A yellow-legged snipe whistled, and, as I answered, almost flew into the shelter. Several times the little humming-bird again buzzed about me. How glad I was to be under canvas once more, with the warm, cheerful fire in front! The barrábara was horrible!

May 27.—In the morning I spread the bear-skins in the open air, labelled all my material, which included specimens of all the species of mammals I could secure, and then started around the shore, three miles from the head of the bay. It was cloudy all day, and there was a drizzling rain very early in the morning. On that side of the island a great quantity of snow still remained, extending more than a foot deep, well below timber line, in some places down nearly to the beach. Just behind my camp was a bald eagle's nest, and the old birds were constantly flying about and crying in alarm, greatly worried to have me so near.

At 6 P. M., when I was at the upper end of the bay, a small sail appeared and entered it, and I at once returned to find Swanson with my men in a small

sloop waiting for me, and with all my material packed
inside. With relief, I learned that the steamer would
not return to Nuchek for four days; therefore I intended to spend the interim, if possible, hunting bears
on Hinchinbrook Island. I had planned to return on
a different steamer, which carries mail and stops once
a month regularly at Nuchek, the *Portland* seldom
stopping there.

We were soon sailing down the bay in a light breeze,
which died out as we came outside and left us in a dead
calm, with a heavy tide-rip against us. We each took
an oar, rowed the sloop seven miles across to Hinchinbrook Island, then six miles around in the back way,
and dropped anchor at two the next morning. It was
now good daylight all night, though in the woods during
the midnight hours a rifle-sight could not be seen.

In the morning I paid my men, who soon left in the
bidarka for Orca, where there is a large trading-store,
to spend the money. I did not see them again. I
visited the Russian priest in the afternoon, and was
not impressed with his appearance or character, and
felt that his chief aim was to utilize the influence gained
over the natives by several generations of ritualistic
training in acquiring furs and money from them. Perhaps other vices could be attributed to him. His duties
extend to all the natives about Prince William Sound.

May 29.—The next day it was raining hard, but
cleared at noon; hence I took a dory and rowed four
miles to the head of the back bay. It was full of the
beautiful harlequin ducks, and I noticed that some of
them were paired. Large flocks were often feeding

out on the beaches and in the water close to shore.
They do not fly very well, and when on the wing keep
uttering a thin *"Creek! Creek!"* Reaching the upper
end of the bay, I went well back in the woods, climbed
a mountain, inspected the slopes about without seeing
any sign of a bear, then returned and began to row back.
When I reached the middle of the bay I saw through
my field-glasses, far in the distance to the left, a small
bear travelling high on a mountain. Immediately I
returned, went three miles through the woods, climbed
the mountain, and observed through my glasses its trail
on the snow, leading from slope to slope until it disappeared, two miles away, over a crest. I thought
the bear was travelling to new feeding-grounds, but it
was too late to follow. Returning to the bay, I rowed
back to Nuchek, intending to start early the next
morning and search all day through the mountains in
the vicinity where I had seen it.

Mrs. Swanson had prepared for me a good meal of
porpoise meat, cut from the porpoise that Misha had
shot as he came back from Montague Island. It was
excellent, tasting more like beef than anything else.

The gulls were now breeding on the rocks in Nuchek
harbor, and swallows were already constructing their
nests under the eaves of the old store. Another northeast storm descended in the night and continued all
the next day until late in the evening, when it cleared.

May 31.—At midnight the whistle of a steamer
aroused us from sleep. We went over on the beach
and found that Captain Linquist, of the *Portland*, had
made a special stop to pick me up, having heard from

Misha, at Orca, that I was waiting. He held the steamer two hours so that I could pack, and I stepped aboard at 3.30 A. M. It was with keen regret that I bade adieu to the Swansons. In every possible way they had done most willingly everything to assist me, even inconveniencing themselves in my behalf, and I enjoyed greatly their warm hospitality.

I had arrived at Nuchek, April 21, and left it May 31. During the interval on Montague Island the state of the weather had permitted only eight and a half days' practical hunting, two days of which, because of not being able to make a landing in new territory, were on disturbed ground where I had already hunted. So in reality I had only six and one-half days of good hunting.

When I awoke, Montague and Hinchinbrook Islands had faded out of sight. There were but five passengers on board. I must record especially the kindness of Captain Linquist, who is considered one of the best captains navigating the coast. He was greatly interested in my trip, and I found him a man with a keen love of nature, and an observer of everything in the wilderness, whenever, in his wide experience on the Asiatic or American coast, he had come in contact with it. He placed his state-room, books, and freedom of the steamer at my disposal, and more than anything else I enjoyed his companionship. I kept the bearskins spread out on deck to give them a final drying, while for three days we steamed down the coast in calm, sunny, perfect weather; along the glorious Saint Elias and Fairweather ranges, then through Icy Strait, and arrived in Juneau on June 2. I boxed all my material, shipped it to the Biological Survey in Washington, and the same evening took a small steamer and arrived in Skagway the next morning, intending to start immediately for the interior to pass the summer in the country adjacent to the upper Pelly River.

All winter my thoughts had turned toward Montague Island and its bears. Now the trip was accomplished and past. But all the incidents and experiences of it still linger with me. The beautiful, calm ocean voyage; the village of Nuchek and its natives; the snow-bound Zaïkof Bay, where the air vibrated musically to the echoing voices of the water-fowl, where sweet bird notes sounded from the woods and the exquisite little humming-bird darted about my camp; the east coast, rock and reef bound, bordered by white breakers and dotted far out from shore by foam from the sea surging over the reefs; the high, rugged, snow-capped mountain ranges; the hilly woods, resplendent glades, deep canyons, gorges, and dashing cascades; the rumble of sliding snow in the mountain-girdled basins overlooking the ocean below; the violent storms, and gloomy, blank days passed in the inhospitable barrábaras; the irresponsible natives; the joyous fulfilment of spring in the wilderness; the bewitching sight of the bears travelling on the high mountain slopes and the interest and excitement of stalking them; all these impressions are deeply graven in my memory. But one stands out still more vividly than all the rest—that sight of the mother bear nursing her moaning cub under the high snow-line of the precipitous slope! Wounded once, she had taken every care of her offspring and lived a life of caution, never descending far from the mountain tops, never dwelling long in one place, and when she rested always concealing herself in high spots difficult of access. But, in spite of all, fate had overtaken her, and she died the very death she had so consciously tried to escape!

THE ELUSIVE CARIBOU OF THE QUEEN
CHARLOTTE ISLANDS, 1906

Caribou on Queen Charlotte Island

Chair once Queen Charlotte

CHAPTER VIII

VIRAGO SOUND

AFTER hunting through the summer and early fall of 1906 on the north side of the Alaska Range, in the vicinity of Mount McKinley, I stopped on my return at Ketchikan, Alaska, October 24, where immediate arrangements were made for a trip to Graham Island—the largest of the Queen Charlotte group—for the purpose of investigating the occurrence of caribou which were supposed to exist there.

The eminent Canadian geologist, Dr. George M. Dawson, made a geological investigation of this group of islands during the summer of 1878 and published a most excellent report, including an appendix on the Haida Indians, in 1880.* He says there is good evidence to show that the wapiti occurs in the northern part of Graham Island. In 1890 he corrected his former suggestion and referred to evidence of caribou instead of wapiti.†

In the year 1880 Alexander Mackenzie, a trader for the Hudson Bay Company at Massett, sent out a fragment of the skull of a caribou with part of the horn attached, averring that the animal had been killed in Virago Sound by an Indian. This imperfect specimen, having passed through several hands, was finally lodged

* Geological Survey of Canada, "Report of Progress for 1878–79." See page 113 B.
† Trans. Royal Soc. Canada, VIII, sec. IV, 51–52.

in the Provincial Museum at Victoria.   In 1900 Ernest
Thompson Seton described it as that of a new species
which he named *Rangifer dawsoni*.   In view of the ·
uncertainty attached to the origin of the specimen and
also of its fragmentary character, other naturalists were
unwilling to accept it as the basis for a new species.

Doubt was increased almost to a certainty after
W. H. Osgood, assistant of the United States Biological
Survey, visited Graham Island in the summer of 1900,
and made a special investigation regarding the supposed Queen Charlotte caribou and the origin of the
particular specimen in the museum at Victoria.   Osgood interviewed the Rev. Mr. Keen, an active natu-
ralist, who had lived at Massett for eight years; Rev.
Mr. Collinson, one of the earliest missionaries at Massett, who had lived there many years, and Mr. Stevens,
who had kept a trading-store there for nine years.   All
were familiar with the story of the "Mackenzie caribou," but none of them believed that the specimen came
originally from the Queen Charlotte Islands, nor did
they believe that caribou had ever existed there.   In
further attempts to trace the story of the type specimen,
Osgood could find no evidence behind it except the word
of the Indians.   The one exception was a communication
from Rev. Charles Harrison, who had come to Massett
as a missionary in 1880, a month after the "Mackenzie
caribou" was reported to have been killed, and who
had partaken of the flesh of the caribou which Mackenzie said he had dried.   Mr. Harrison in his communication also mentioned more recent evidence given by
Indians, who said they had seen caribou near Virago

Sound, and he expressed confidence not only in the genuineness of the "Mackenzie caribou," but also in the present existence of caribou on Graham Island. Mr. Harrison's evidence, however, was second-hand, and naturalists paid little attention to it, but considered that the case had been practically discredited.

Four or five years later the United States Biological Survey began to receive new evidence of such a character that the whole matter needed reconsideration. Osgood's report had finally reached Mr. Harrison at Massett, and in December, 1904, he sent two half-breed Indians into the woods tributary to Virago Sound. They spent only a day and night, but on their return reported having seen large tracks and brought some dung of a large-hoofed animal.

In March, 1905, Mr. Harrison himself and the Rev. H. A. Collinson, the missionary stationed at Massett, who was the son of the Mr. Collinson interviewed by Osgood, took five Indians and spent ten days in the woods near Virago Sound. They reported that they saw abundant caribou tracks and dung and picked up some caribou hair.

The following April Henry Edenshaw, son of a former chief of the Haidas, went into the same country and likewise said that he saw tracks and dung.

Shortly after this Captain Hunt, of the British navy, went into the same woods for a short time, and not only saw the tracks but found a shed caribou horn.

In March, 1906, Messrs. Harrison and Collinson again attempted to find a caribou, and penetrating the woods from the north coast six miles below Virago

Sound, they crossed through the country to the sound. They found caribou tracks very scarce until they reached the area in which they had before hunted, where the tracks were still abundant.

All these facts were received by the Biological Survey, and the eminent naturalists attached to it were startled, to say the least. The habitat of the genus *Rangifer* is somewhat similar the world over—the dry interior of the north and, wherever land occurs, over nearly the whole arctic region. That caribou should live and exist in the Queen Charlotte Islands, a very humid country, so absolutely different in character and climate from their habitat as known up to this time, appeared so extraordinary that Dr. Merriam, the chief of the Biological Survey, sought for more evidence from somebody personally known to him, and therefore asked me to go to Virago Sound and penetrate the woods where tracks were reported to have been seen.

My arrival in Ketchikan was fortunately coincident with that of B. F. Graham, who was largely interested in timber lands around Massett Inlet, and was making a trip there to inspect them. Together we negotiated successfully with Captain Thompson and engaged him to take us over there in his small schooner *Urius*, which had been fitted with a gasoline auxiliary. Having purchased provisions in Ketchikan, I boarded the boat at midnight, October 25, and cramped myself into a miserable little bunk next to the gasoline engine just before the captain gave orders to start.

October 26.—In the morning we were passing through

Dixon's Entrance and soon the little schooner was toss-
ing in a heavy southeast storm.   Graham and the men
accompanying him were very sea-sick, and the fumes
from the gasoline had given me a very bad headache.
In a drenching rain I remained on deck for five hours,
when we entered a fog and soon found that the captain,
having steered out of his course, had entered Virago
Sound.   We headed up against the wind for eight
miles, passed Massett, and continued three miles up
the inlet, where the anchor was thrown over and we
were rowed to the shore.   A mile's walk brought us to
Delcatla, the residence of Charles Harrison, who kindly
volunteered to give me the benefit of his experience
and to assist me in arranging for the hunt.

Mr. Harrison, a Scotchman, and formerly a missionary for twenty years among the Haidas at Massett,
speaks the native language fluently, and knows more
about Graham Island than any other man.   He had
for some time been living on his ranch, where he had
cleared and cultivated a great deal of land, besides
gathering a band of cattle which ranged for some distance about *Delcatla*, and found there abundant food not
only to sustain themselves but to increase in numbers.
The Canadian Government had appointed Mr. Harrison
revenue collector at Massett, which is a port of entry.
His personal acquaintance with the Massett Indians is
so sympathetic that he not only knows them individ-
ually better than others do, but also has more influence
with them.   His wife, a fine Englishwoman, received us
with charming hospitality, and in such a congenial
atmosphere we soon recovered from the effects of the

disagreeable trip on the schooner and passed a comfortable night.

October 27.—There was a heavy rain-storm in the morning, but in the afternoon it cleared, although occasionally a light shower fell. In the morning I went on the schooner, and, unloading all my provisions, placed them in an old abandoned house on the shore. After lunch, Mr. Harrison saddled horses and we rode through the woods toward Massett, passing over a good trail, through a luxuriant forest, where the giant spruces were richly festooned with hanging green moss and adorned with beautiful ferns growing on their trunks and lower branches. The little winter wrens again appeared; the flicker passed in wavy flight among the trees; the bald eagle was flying about and ravens were very numerous. After three miles of that delightful ride we reached Massett, the Haida Indian village.

It consists of a main street bordered by low houses, and along it were many old totem-posts which, together with the typical Haida canoes, both large and small, pulled up on the beach, stamp Massett impressively with a display of the culture of the coast Indians. Most of the Indians, although under the influence of missionaries for thirty or more years, still preserved the typical characteristics of their race, and were superior in physique to any of the coast Indians whom I had before seen anywhere between Vancouver Island and Yakutat, Alaska.

Riding to the house of the Rev. W. E. Collinson, we discussed my coming campaign in search of the caribou, and later went to visit the Indian, Henry Edenshaw,

Photograph by W. H. Osgood.   By permission of U. S. Biological Survey.

Spruce on the Queen Charlotte Islands.

who gave me all the information he could. I decided first to hunt in the country about Virago Sound, particularly in that part of the woods where so many signs had been seen, and if no caribou should be killed there, to direct my later movements according to my own judgment.

October 28.—A southeast storm, beginning in the night and continuing all the next day, compelled me to remain at *Delcatla.* I had employed a half-breed, Robert Brown, and Mr. Harrison's son, Percy, to accompany me on the trip. Robert was a strong, stalwart fellow, capable of doing plenty of hard labor, but the Indian part of his nature so predominated that he was always glad to shirk. Percy, a young man of twenty, was active, energetic, and capable. From beginning to end he willingly did everything he could to help me and to make the trip a success.

October 29.—In the morning, after the arrival of Robert Brown at *Delcatla*, we loaded a large Haida canoe and started for Massett. It was raining so hard that on our arrival in the village Robert was glad to believe that the sea was too rough outside the inlet to make a start, and I deposited my provisions in a house, lunched with Henry Edenshaw, and spent part of the afternoon visiting many Indians and discussing the caribou question. I found that all were familiar with the fact that tracks were abundant near Virago Sound, but none with whom I talked had seen a track, nor did the Haidas have any traditions about the animal. Elthkeega, an old Indian, then dead, had owned a few dogs that would chase the bear, and I learned that those dogs once drove a caribou bull and cow into Virago Sound, both of which Elthkeega had killed. That bull was the "Mackenzie caribou."

Those who read this narrative will wonder how it could be possible that these Indians had never seen a caribou on the island. I also still wonder at it. The Indians have always gone into the interior along the rivers, to set traps for bears or martens, also to get trees for their canoes, and occasionally they have crossed the island to the west coast. One had been accustomed to go over to Lake Jal-un to trap, and had even constructed a house there. But, except along the rivers, they seldom went far back in the woods. Since there are no deer or other game animals on the island, except the bear, which they only trap, the Haidas have never been big-game hunters. Most of them have been afraid to go far back from the shore by reason of their superstitions—their traditions alleging that "monsters, hobgoblins, spirits," etc., haunt the interior woods, and besides, until Mr. Harrison tried to interest them, there was no inducement for them to hunt for the caribou. The whole village became greatly excited about my hunt, and some of the Indians openly expressed contempt for a white man as a hunter.

October 30.—Percy and I walked back to *Delcatla*, where we spent the night, and the next morning made an early start for Massett, where we found Robert Brown still sleeping. The sky was clear, and at nine-forty-five we had loaded all our provisions into the boat —a small sloop of the Columbia River type—and were ready for our trip. Soon after leaving Massett Inlet

Photograph by W. H. Osgood.   By permission of U. S. Biological Survey

The shore of an inlet of the Queen Charlotte Islands.

we passed the abandoned Indian village Yan, which then appeared like a small forest of totem-posts; the grave of a former devil-doctor, constructed on a high reef, well out from the shore, was pointed out to me. We had a delightful sail in a fair wind to Virago Sound. Great numbers of ducks, pelagic cormorants, and geese were flying about on all sides, and the surf dashing against the rocky shores made a white line against the forest background.

Beating against a strong tide, we finally entered Virago Sound and anchored in a small bay near the Indian village of Kung, which had been abandoned some time before, the residents having moved to Massett. They still occupied it occasionally, however, when they were trapping or fishing near the sound. A number of fine totem-posts were scattered about, and parts of the old communal house were still standing. Four families of Indians were there, temporarily occupying houses more recently constructed. Mr. Harrison had told me that the Kung Indians had never imitated the Christian religion—which was not true of the other Haidas on the Queen Charlotte Islands.

Unloading the boat, we moved everything into a small, leaking, abandoned house, while the Indians gathered around us, much excited about the object of my trip. Among them were old Glower and his wife —both typical, and representing the best of the older Haidas. Glower, having accompanied Messrs. Harrison and Collinson on their trip for caribou, gave me all the information about the country that he could, but little of it was pertinent to finding caribou.

CHAPTER IX

SEARCHING FOR CARIBOU

October 31.—Robert Brown and I started the next morning to make a reconnoissance back in the woods, at first walking two miles down the beach. It was calm though cloudy; bald eagles were plentiful, numerous gulls were screaming, and shore birds in great numbers were restlessly feeding along the water's edge. We entered the woods, and I found myself again in a dark, dripping forest composed of enormous spruces, hemlocks, cedars, and balsams, rising from a dense growth of sallal, salmon-berry, and huckleberry. Everywhere throughout the woods the sallal grows large and very dense, much more dense than I had seen it on Vancouver Island. Its large leaves are so shaped as to hold water, and when walking through it, in or after rain, one receives a soaking comparable only with a complete immersion in water. Dense sallal is the most characteristic feature of the woods about Virago Sound, although the huckleberry is almost as dense. Both occur abundantly in the woods and are not so much confined to swamps as on Vancouver Island. Beginning at the shore, the surface is most uneven and irregular, rising in two or three ridges of several hundred feet in height, to a gently rolling plateau which extends many miles back, and here and there is cut by deep ravines through which the creeks flow.

Totem posts at Kung.   October 31.

Ruins of old Communal House at Kung.   October 31.

We struggled up and down to the plateau, where we found ourselves in a large glade, the surface of which was swampy and filled with small depressions full of water. In these open swamps Mr. Harrison had seen the tracks of caribou. We pushed on through woods and

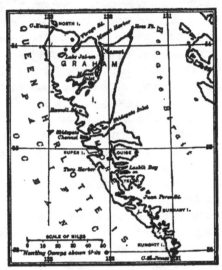

Map of Queen Charlotte Islands.

glades, but without seeing a sign, until one o'clock in the afternoon when we lunched. We then resumed the tramp and in about an hour reached a glade of several hundred acres, where I saw, passing for sixty yards along the edge of the woods, *the distinct tracks of a caribou.* Soon I found some dung which did not appear to be old, and it was an intense satisfaction to realize at last that the caribou on Graham Island were not imaginary.

Signs of their existence were there before my eyes, written on the ground beneath me. Being four miles distant from the shore, we did not have time to pursue our search further. Since Robert Brown had lost all sense of direction, I took a course by my compass and led the way through the woods. Becoming frightened before long, he climbed several trees in the hope of seeing the sound, but I insisted that we were travelling in the right direction, and kept it in spite of his objections until, as it grew dark, light broke through the trees ahead, and we suddenly came to the beach near Kung.

The result of that day was encouraging. The existence of caribou had been demonstrated, and although I realized that it would be next to impossible to see one in the woods, there was a chance to do so in the open swamps. The fine Queen Charlotte jay with conspicuous crest was abundant, also winter wrens and varied thrushes.

The mammal life* of the Queen Charlotte Islands is interesting from the fact that more new species have been evolved there than in the other islands of British Columbia and Alaska. The black bear, *Ursus carlottæ*, has developed different skull characters; the marten, *Mustela nesophila;* land-otter, *Lutra canadensis periclyzomæ;* the weasel, *Putorius haidarum*, and eight other species of indigenous land mammals—shrews, mice, and bats, including all known to occur on the islands—have been described as new. Some genera common in the mainland, such as deer, minks,

---

* "Natural History of the Queen Charlotte Islands," by W. H. Osgood (North American Fauna No. 21), Washington, 1901.

beavers, wolves, foxes, squirrels, and the mice *Microtus* and *Evotomys*, do not exist on the islands. The variety in bird life is of course limited in November, but I observed much more in the interior here than on Vancouver Island.

Judging from my experience among caribou in Alaska and the Yukon Territory, it seemed apparent that a band must be roaming somewhere. I called in Glower and the other Indians, all of whom knew more about the Virago Sound country than the other Haidas, and through Robert Brown as interpreter held a long though unsatisfactory conference with them. I employed Glower, who told me he could take me all through the area covered by Messrs. Harrison and Collinson. The Indians said that there were some high mountains beyond Lake Jal-un, which was six miles inland from the head of the sound, and one of the boys, Tommy by name, told me that he had been to the lake with his father, who had blazed a trail to the Jal-un River, where there was an old canoe in which I could paddle up to the lake. In case no caribou were found below in the plateau country, which should be explored first, it seemed to me quite necessary to go to those mountains and investigate the higher country. For the purpose of deciding the location of a camp, I arranged to have Glower show me the section with which he was familiar. Since the Indians had plenty of dried halibut and an abundance of fine, large boiled crabs, I fared well that night before sleeping.

November 1.—It was cloudy the next day, but there was no rain, and Glower, Robert, and I with heavy packs started early, plunged into the woods and struggled up over the ridges, pushing through the dripping sallal for three hours until we reached a point on the edge of a swamp, where Glower decided to camp. I was then in the same part of the country where the others had hunted and where Captain Hunt had found the shed horn. We had passed through the swamp where I had seen the tracks the day before and had reached some large swamps beyond. As we lunched, a flock of geese flew over, just clearing the tall trees as they passed by, honking; a flock of chickadees were flitting near among the trees, while the tap of a woodpecker sounded not far away. Soon a familiar whistling call sounded high in the heavens, and looking up I saw the V-shaped wedge of a flock of little brown cranes passing southeast.

Taking my rifle, I went out in the swamp and, following the edge of the woods, proceeded with caution, continually pausing to look and listen. A few old caribou tracks were all along the edge, and here and there indistinct trails extending for short distances to the woods, where all signs of tracks faded out. The dung was old and so were all the tracks. Occasionally tracks crossed the swamp, but nearly all were close to the woods.

It was somewhat difficult to find my way back to camp, where I arrived just before dark to see my shelter tent already erected and a fine log fire blazing in front. The sky was clear above and the sparks shooting up among the great trees were often confused with the stars seen through the branches. The men had ceased chatting and I was waiting for sleep to obliterate my eagerness for the morrow's hunt; the embers of the fire were still glowing brightly; branches of the giant trees were indistinctly visible against the starlit sky, and the silence of the vast forest had cast its mysterious spell about us, when there sounded, far off in the darkness, a metallic, trumpet-like note, becoming louder as it approached nearer and nearer until directly overhead; then gradually it grew fainter and fainter, finally dying away in the distance, and again all was still. After an interval the same experience was repeated, another note sounded and continued along the same course; then an interval, and another; then silence, and I fell asleep. They were the voices of swans flying over the forest.

November 2.—At daylight Glower and I had started. It was clear and calm all day. Slowly we walked through the swamp, crossed through a patch of woods and circled around another swamp of several hundred acres, where we flushed three English snipes. After forcing our way through half a mile of woods, we entered a larger swamp, walked around it, and rested to eat some lunch. Old caribou tracks were common everywhere around the forest's edges, but we seldom saw one even a short distance away from the woods. We tramped through woods for a mile and a half more before we emerged into a large expanse of open swamp, where old tracks and dung were still more abundant, but always near the edge. In places a faint trail was indicated. As we were then beyond the country where the others had hunted, I decided to move my camp there and remain to search for caribou.

November 3.—We returned to camp and, burdening our shoulders with packs, started early the next morning, Glower taking the lead, to find the place I had selected the day before. To my surprise he began to circle in the woods and was soon completely lost. After sending Robert up several trees for the purpose of marking the more open country, he finally decided to take a northeast direction, but as I had carefully watched my compass the preceding day and knew that the right direction was southwest, I insisted that they should follow me. They finally consented to do so. The day was fine and the woods dry, but the heavy loads made progress slow and toilsome. About noon we reached the camping-place and temporarily put up the shelter. After lunch Robert and Glower departed for Kung in quest of provisions, and I started out to spend the afternoon hunting.

Travelling in a southeast direction, I passed swamp after swamp, carefully watching and listening at the edge of the woods; but although old tracks and weak trails were everywhere visible close to the woods, no animal appeared.

This open country should be described as a succession of *swamp-barrens*. Extending a great many miles, perhaps the whole length of Graham Island, they have a trend northeast and southwest. They are covered in spots with caribou lichen-moss, grass, and weeds. Small bull pines and occasional cedars are scattered over them. Though there is a vast stretch of barrens in the directions mentioned, the dense woods irregularly intersect them at varying intervals in such a manner

A swamp-barren west of Virago Sound.   November 3.

Another swamp-barren west of Virago Sound.   Glower at left, Robert
Brown at right.   November 4.

as to make great clear spaces, connected by open lanes through the forest, rather than continuous open country. Some of the barrens, varying in width from a few yards up to half a mile or more, exceed a mile in length; others are circular in shape; others quite irregular. Narrow strips of woods often intersect them in different directions, and it is very confusing to find one's way among them, or locate any given spot. All are dotted with depressions filled with water, varying from a yard in diameter to miniature lakes. A strip of woods a few yards in width, where the undergrowth is not so dense and the ground is hard, usually borders their edges. Elsewhere the surface is one vast swamp of muddy ground, which renders the walking particularly disagreeable. These barrens are fairly level, and between variations in altitude the inclines are gradual, never abrupt. Scarcely anything resembling a hill exists in them.

On and near the barrens, everywhere in the vicinity of Virago Sound, firewood is abundant. Sound, dead trees—spruces, hemlocks, and cedars—were everywhere, and the dead bull pine is as fine wood for burning as any that exists in the northern country. On the whole, the conditions for camping were much superior to those on many of the islands in the northern Pacific, for the reason that wood for fire is so abundant and so easy to obtain.

In spite of the difficulties, it was fascinating to hunt for that illusive caribou which no white man had ever seen. It was there somewhere, and the task of solving the mystery of its whereabouts sustained my in-

terest. Too much eagerness caused me to forget the
time, until rain and approaching darkness warned me
that I had gone too far. Taking a northeast course,
I started back, and before long it was dark; but I kept
on going blindly by compass, every now and then light-
ing matches to see the needle. Hour after hour I proceeded, feeling my way with a staff, until at eleven in
the night it was evident that I could not recognize the
spot where the shelter was erected unless I should come
very close to it.

Going into the woods and groping around, I fortunately found an old decayed stump from which I could
tear great slabs of wood which were dry on the inside.
I then found a large spruce tree and succeeded in light-
ing a fire against it. The light of the fire assisted me
in finding several logs, which were soon thrown on.
Then, breaking some cedar branches, I heaped them
up in front of the fire sufficiently high to keep me off
the wet ground, and, between intervals of rising to
replenish the fire, caught snatches of sleep in spite of a
pouring rain.

November 4.—When it dawned I went out into the
open swamp and recognized my camp three hundred
yards ahead. Quickly reaching it, I soon had some
bacon cooked, which with bread and tea refreshed me
so much that two hours of sleep was sufficient to rest
me, and I started again, taking, this time, a more westerly course and maintaining it until it was time to turn
back. Caribou tracks occurred about the same as in
other directions, all old and close to the woods, only now
and then crossing the narrow parts of the barrens.

There was no evidence of an abundance of the animals, the indications being that not more than one or two caribou had been together at any time, though occasionally the track of a calf was observed with the others. It rained hard all that day, and, with the exception of caribou and occasional bear tracks, not a sign of mammal life appeared in the woods or on the barrens. Jays, chestnut-backed chickadees, Oregon juncos, bald eagles, and ravens were common.

On my return, Robert, Percy, Glower, and another Indian, George, were sitting before the fire, and the camp was stocked with a fair supply of provisions. I had traversed the barrens from near the coast to my camp, and also to the west, as far as they continued, but had not seen any fresh signs of caribou.

November 5.—Glower and George left at daylight for Kung. Percy and I started over the barrens to cover as much of the area that I had already traversed as possible during daylight, and to see if any fresh caribou tracks had been made. It was a beautiful clear morning, but at noon rain began to fall and by night a heavy northeast storm had set in. We proceeded rapidly, looking for fresh tracks rather than for the animals, and finally returned to camp, having covered many miles, but without having observed any fresh signs.

During our absence, Robert had reconstructed the camp. We had been lying on cedar boughs thrown on soft, muddy ground. He had placed logs side by side, over a surface large enough to serve for sleeping space, and had put on them sufficient boughs for a bed; he had also laid logs along the ground so that we could walk outside without sinking in mud and water. He had split out numerous rough planks from cedar-trees which had been felled, and had placed them upright around the front of the shelter in such a way that they served as a barrier against wind and rain.

November 6.—Another clear day found Percy and myself travelling rapidly southwest, without pausing to hunt until we passed the limits of the barrens which I had already investigated. Here we entered the woods, descended a deep ravine, and, after crossing a good-sized creek, ascended half a mile to the barrens beyond. In some gravel bordering the creek I noticed the old imprints of a caribou's forefeet and along the creek was also a well-defined bear trail.

We hunted with great caution all day about the barrens, and found the conditions the same—old caribou tracks near the edge of the woods, but not any sign that was fresh. Imprints were never visible in the woods so that wandering about in them was useless, as the sallal was so large and dense that any caribou would have been frightened away long before one could get near enough to see it. In addition to the other birds mentioned, I saw a flock of golden-crowned kinglets, and noticed several flocks of geese feeding about the barrens, and also bald eagles, which were constantly soaring across.

One conspicuous feature of the atmospheric effect in that locality was an optical delusion exactly the reverse of that common on our Western plains of the United States. Objects appeared very distant when

Glower and his wife at Kung.   November 8.

Old Indian grave at Kung.   November 23.

they were really very near, and it required a long time
to become accustomed to the short spaces actually
traversed when to the vision they appeared so long.

I had now wandered over so much of the open country within reach of the camp without seeing a fresh
track that it was quite clear to me the caribou were
then either remaining exclusively in the woods or had
retired to the mountainous country farther back, beyond the Jal-un River. I therefore decided to return
to Kung the next day and make all possible haste to
reach the mountains near Lake Jal-un.

November 7.—Though it rained all night, the following day was clear, and we took down the shelter,
made up our packs, and plunged into the dripping
sallal, travelling directly east. In six hours we reached
the beach not far from Kung, and after cooking supper went over to Glower's house to spend the evening. In his large house, ten or twelve Indians—men,
women, and children—were sitting around a fire in the
centre eating some crabs which had just been boiled.
Dried halibut was hanging on all the walls and fresh
ones were hung to dry on poles above the fire. Glower
and his wife were seated at one end of the fire, apparently presiding over a feast. A granddaughter of
Glower, a pretty Indian girl of sixteen, was playing
with her baby, which was at least a year old. Alas!
its fair skin bore evidence that the mother's experience
had been that of most of those young unmarried Haida
girls who are subjected to contact with white men
in the salmon cannery near Ketchikan, where nearly
all are employed at work during the summer.

Glower assumed some dignity as my host, and after listening to my experience in trying to find a caribou, began to talk in the clucking Haida language. Soon he quite forgot my presence and launched into excited speech accompanied with violent gestures. The others sat around him in a circle, listening in rapt attention for two hours, and responding to his climaxes with grunts of approval. From Robert I learned that he was relating a mythical tale, handed down from generation to generation among the Kung tribe—a story of the origin of Virago Sound. The excitement of the listeners and their intense interest in the tale indicated quite clearly, in spite of long contact with the teachings of missionaries, their belief in their own mythology.

As we walked around the beach to our little house, there was not a ripple on the water of the bay, not a sound but the screaming of gulls and occasional quacking of ducks. A rich salt odor pervaded the air, and I lingered awhile outside before going in to sleep.

CHAPTER X

LAKE JAL-UN

November 8.—In the morning we found that in some way a spark had lodged in the canvas sail which was just outside the house and several large holes had been burnt in it. I employed two Indian girls to repair it, but it was noon before they had finished. After loading the boat, we rowed to the head of the west bay in the sound and put up the shelter in a grove of big hemlocks. The day was clear, and while moving up the bay I had looked in vain for that big bare mountain near Lake Jal-un which the Indians told me could be seen from the sound. Tommy Mark, the son of the Indian who had blazed a trail to the lake, had refused to go, but had told us where to find the blazes. Robert also had pretended to know the country. I had noticed that he was becoming tired of the trip and his only thought had been to get back to Kung, where he could sit about, smoke, and chat. Later I realized that he had hoped I would be discouraged about the Lake Jal-un trip and would finally give up looking for more caribou.

November 9.—As we could find no blazes the next morning, Robert and I walked three miles around the bay to some Indian houses, then occupied by two families, located at the mouth of the Naden River. There was a heavy storm all day. The bay was full of ducks, and the air whistled with the wing-beats of numerous golden-eyes; flocks of geese were feeding on the bars and flying low around the points; great flocks of crows were feeding on the beaches, and thousands of shore birds were flying about, as well as numerous gulls, while bald eagles were everywhere.

The Indians at Naden River had been trapping bears and land-otters, and also building a cedar canoe. They had trapped one bear and one otter, the skulls of both of which I purchased. They knew nothing about the interior country away from the Naden River. I rented a canoe from them, and, after returning in it to my shelter, sent Robert back to Kung with a liberal offer for Tommy Mark to return with him and guide us to the lake. In the afternoon I climbed the ridges and, reaching the barrens, walked around the edges, but did not see a single caribou track.

November 10.—At eight in the morning Robert returned with Tommy, who, although a big, strapping fellow, was reputed to be the laziest and most worthless of all the Haidas in Massett. We made up our packs and followed up the bank of the river which enters the west bay without finding the blazes which Tommy and the Indians had told me began at the mouth of the river. We travelled on a well-beaten bear trail for a mile before the first blaze appeared, and then followed the blazed trees up over ridges, through dense woods, until, at 1.30 P. M., we emerged on the barrens. The rain had begun to fall soon after we started and it continued in a heavy downpour all day. The barrens were a continuation of those I had hunted over farther to the northeast, but were much wider and vaster in extent. After making tea and taking some lunch, we resumed our tramp, with shoulders aching under the heavy packs, until 4 P. M., when we reached the Jal-un River. While crossing the barrens I had carefully looked for caribou tracks, but not a single one did I see.

We found the Jal-un River very deep, with a sluggish current, and from forty to a hundred feet wide. Tommy pulled out from the brush a small cedar canoe, which was thoroughly rotten and had a crack extending diagonally across it but not quite deep enough to admit the water. We cramped ourselves into it and paddled up the river, which was so full of snags and fallen trees that some of them had to be chopped out to clear a passage; twice we were compelled to portage the canoe around log-jams. Once, while trying to pass the canoe under a log, the top of the bow snapped off, but we kept on, and, after paddling two miles more, entered the lake and found a miserable little hut leaking everywhere except in one corner. We made a fire in the centre of the hut, which, except for a perpendicular space of two feet from the ground, soon filled with smoke, and we were obliged to keep our heads below to avoid it. Cramped in a corner, we passed a restless night, and the next morning dawned clear.

November 11.—At daybreak Tommy and I paddled to the head of the lake and started for the highest mountain beyond. It was an exquisite little sheet of water a mile and a half long and almost as wide.

Buried in high mountains rising abruptly from the shores, it resembled closely an Adirondack lake. But the magnificent forest, surrounding it with big trees which, richly festooned with mosses and lichens, inclined over the water around the shores, gave to it an impressive beauty quite its own.

At first we tramped up along the inlet, a fair-sized creek full of coho salmon, floundering and splashing about the pools. Numerous bear trails led from the mountain-sides down to the creek, and abundant fresh remains of salmon indicated that several bears were still feeding there. In some of their dung I noticed round worms. We fought our way along the side of a steep ridge and at last reached the slopes of the mountain. Not only sallal, but devil's-club and salmon-berry, were so dense that the tramping was even more difficult than about the woods near Virago Sound. Tommy was in despair when, after lunch, he saw that I persisted in climbing; but he followed me until within three hundred yards of the top, where the slope was very steep and covered with dense, small salmon-berry bush, reminding me of the slopes on Montague Island. Here he waited in a secluded spot, while I kept on and reached the top.

The east wind was very strong and it was misty toward the south. The mountain I was on dominated all others as far as I could see, and was about five thousand feet high. Its top was covered with grass and here and there were small patches of stunted spruce. After so many days of wandering about the flat country near Virago Sound, the view from the top

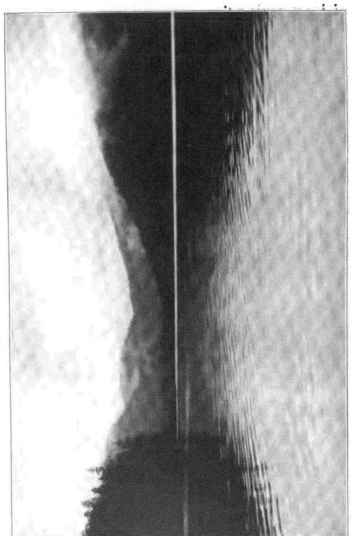

Lake Jal-un. November 11.

was inspiring. It was clear toward the north and
west, and the whole country was visible—a vast, rolling, forest-clad area reaching to the north coast, where
North Island loomed up in the sea beyond.

The west coast was almost below me, and the miles
of white breakers and foaming reefs reminded me of
the east coast of Montague Island. To the south it
was mountainous as far as I could see, while toward
the east were the barrens scattered in a well-defined
northerly direction among the woods.

I walked all over the top and along the slopes where
the ground was sufficiently hard to retain the tracks
of any animals large enough to make an impression
on the surface. Bear tracks and diggings, made in
the spring, were abundant; but not a sign of caribou
did I see. Had any caribou been about there within
a year, I would undoubtedly have seen some sign of
them. When it began to rain, I joined Tommy, and we
started on our long, tiresome tramp to the lake, which
was reached just at dark when the wind and rain had
increased to a violent storm.

I have seldom attempted any kind of boating with
more misgiving, or with a feeling of more danger, than
when we took our seats in that little rotten canoe and
began to paddle through the darkness, against wind,
choppy, white-capped waves, and beating rain. Any
moment the canoe was likely to break in two, and twice
we had to land and bail it out. But we reached the
little house safely and, after taking food and tea, again
passed a restless night, lying in pools of water made
by the rain beating in through the top and sides.

My disappointment was very keen, as I had quite counted on finding caribou in the higher country; but it was clear that none ranged there at any time, and also that even the barrens we had crossed the day before were beyond the limits of their tracks. My only remaining resource was to return at once to Kung and keep hunting about the country where I had seen the signs. ·

November 12.—The next day a raging southeast storm kept us huddled in the hut all day. It brought back vividly the similar blank days that I had endured on Montague Island. Robert, who had been defeated in his purpose to keep me from going to Lake Jal-un, was ugly and sullen, scarcely speaking all day. Tommy was always content to do nothing and smoke the tobacco I had given him; but Percy was cheerful and companionable, and had been so much interested in the object of my trip that he shared my disappointment as well as my ambition to continue the hunt.

November 13.—Through rain and fog we risked our lives in that canoe, as it floated swiftly down among the entangled logs of the river, which had risen four feet and was racing swiftly. But we reached the trail, and trudged along under our packs for five hours, until we arrived at the sound, where we found our boat high and dry at low tide and were obliged to pass the night in the woods. The open air and the big fire throwing up sparks among the trees made a pleasant contrast to the smoky, leaking little house where we had passed the last three nights.

November 14.—Leaving at high tide the next day, we slowly sailed in a heavy rain to Kung, to find that

En route for Lake Jal-un.   Robert Brown, Percy, and Tommy.
November 10.

Southwest from a mountain peak near Lake Jal-un.   November 11.

a portion of our provisions stored in our house had been pilfered, probably by the Haida girls and boys.

November 15.—We passed the night sleeping among several Indians in Glower's house, and the next day again established camp in our old quarters in the barrens. It was the only part of the country where I had seen caribou signs, and for the few days that remained, until the arrival of the *Urius*, which, by agreement, was due on November 23, I intended to search as thoroughly as possible in all directions.

November 16.—That night, for the first time, there was a hard frost, and at daylight I was off when all the surface was white and the little ponds were covered with thin ice. It was a beautiful day, and, tramping all about the edges of the barrens, I kept entering the woods and going back into the little glades. Had there been a fresh track I must have seen it on the frosty ground. But only the old ones, then quite familiar to me, were visible. It was after dark when I reached camp and found Robert again sullen and threatening to return to Kung.

November 17.—The following day was clear and balmy, and I hurried across the barrens, crossed the creek to the south, and tramped all day over the country in that direction, seeking spots that had been overlooked before, and often entering the woods to watch and listen. The old tracks were there as before, but no new one appeared. I had noticed many times that near the old tracks the moss had been dug up in spots; but having also seen it thus turned over where there were no tracks, I concluded it must have been done by a bear.

November 18.—The next morning I went northeast to the end of the barrens, and, crossing two miles through the woods, hunted in the northwest limits. In that direction old tracks became gradually scarcer, until they entirely disappeared. A heavy storm descended at noon, and I did not reach camp until long after dark.

November 19.—On the following day, which was clear until the early afternoon, when another storm descended, I tramped about the edges of the barrens until dark without result.

November 20.—The next day, after a light snow had fallen in the night, I went across the creek and hunted all day, but not a fresh sign was seen. I did, however, see a fresh track of a bear that had crossed the barren.

Black bears were exceedingly abundant on Graham Island, and I might easily have killed one near Lake Jal-un, where they were feeding on salmon, above the inlet. In places along the edge of the barrens, I often saw faint bear trails, and here and there a lightly beaten trail would cross; but the deep, well-defined trails always follow both sides of the salmon rivers. The trails elsewhere always lead to the rivers. The Indians told me that bears "go home"—that is, to hibernate—in early December and come out again in March. They first appear nearer the beaches in April. Judging by the signs I saw on the mountains near the lake, they evidently keep pretty high above timber for a while after they leave winter quarters, where they dig out mice and eat grass and roots. The natives say that the bears do not eat the sockeye salmon which begin to run up the rivers in May and June, but until September, when the other salmon run, they remain in the woods or among the hills and near the beaches, eating roots and berries.

The natives always trap bears along the rivers, constructing deadfalls and rope snares, though a few use steel traps.   Bears are particularly abundant along the whole west coast, where the natives never molest them. The Massett Indians were then trapping from thirty to sixty bears a year, and four years before my visit eighty skins had been brought in—one season's catch.   The skins had gone down so much in value that a great many of the Indians had ceased to trap for them at all.   Undoubtedly, since the timber industry on Graham Island has been opened up and has given the natives as much employment as they want, they will in the future take less and less interest in the difficult task of trapping bears; perhaps they may cease altogether.   I learned from them that the animal is as timid on these islands as black bears are everywhere else on the continent.

November 21.—One more day was left for hunting, and it was beautiful and clear.   An hour before daylight, Percy and I started and walked, without pausing, to the south.   Passing the last barren where I had hunted up to that time, we resumed the hunt with caution.   Old tracks were still visible near the woods, but kept getting rarer the farther toward the south we went, until a point was reached where there were no tracks at all.   We were eight miles southwest of camp and not far from where we had crossed the barrens when going to the Jal-un River. Turning back, we still hunted carefully along the edges, but night came on rapidly and long after dark we reached camp.

November 22.—The next day, as we were bringing our packs to Kung, through a heavy rain-storm, we received our last soaking—to be wet through was a condition that had long before become our normal state during a tramp in the woods. That day I saw a sooty grouse sitting on the limb of a tree, the only one seen during the whole trip. As the wind and the tide were against us, we remained at Kung and passed the night in Glower's house.

My caribou hunt had ended. During the whole trip my rifle had not been cocked. I had not even seen a living mammal, though I had completely circled the area within which old caribou tracks were visible. The only tangible result of my trip was to bring back a small bottle of dung as proof that caribou were really there. It was clear that the tracks I had seen indicated very few caribou and that these kept mostly in the woods skirting the edges of the barrens. Or, if the caribou had moved from that area, they must have travelled through the woods where their hoofs made no impressions on the surface—at least none were visible there.

November 23.—The next day was clear and absolutely calm, and Percy and I took the oars and rowed until dark, when we reached Massett.

On Vancouver Island I had suffered from rain, storm, and fog; had fought against the dense undergrowth

The old Haida, Joshua, at Kung.   November 23.

Susan, old Haida woman, at Kung.   November 23.

and pushed through swamps, yet I had found variety
in the landscape. Streams dashed over precipitous
slopes in fine cascades; big stretches of clear forest
harbored deer that looked curiously at me or stole
quietly away; red squirrels frisked about and chattered, and occasionally the wapiti appeared. Difficulties and experiences of a somewhat different character I had had on Montague Island. I was constantly in the midst of wonderful landscapes, bounded
here by mountains, there by the ocean, while success
with the bears added zest and pleasure to each day's
work. But here, in the woods of the Queen Charlotte
Islands, how different! Except for one day among the
scenery about Lake Jal-un, my experience was made
up of carrying a pack through dense sallal, or continually tramping, slop, slop, slop, through a monotonous
level barren waste, most of the time through rain and
storm, and not once having a sight of mammal life to
enliven the dreary wilderness and give the wild woods
their true charm. Yet, even after such a complete
failure among dismal surroundings, I felt keen regret
at leaving. The repeated monotony of the hunt was
in some degree compensated for by the continual crav-
ing to see one of those mysterious caribou which I
knew were there. The hunting was in the open and
my senses were constantly keyed to a high pitch as
each bit of new territory came within the field of my
strained vision. The eagerness, ever present, suddenly to behold that coveted caribou on the edge of
the woods had become a habit which I was loath to
relinquish.

Possibilities of roaming about the west coast along its rock-bound shores, among very old remnants of Haida villages, where bears are abundant and where even a few sea-otters sometimes still come in on the reefs near Frederick Island, were attractive. Again, the waters of Virago Sound, where water-fowl were so abundant and the air was perfumed with a strong salt odor, were peculiarly fascinating, while the Haida Indians—the most picturesque of all I had seen on the northern coast—were interesting both to see and to associate with when they were in their old original haunts away from Massett.

All the conditions on the Queen Charlotte Islands are suitable as a habitat for the Sitka deer, *Odocoileus columbianus sitkensis*, and the government of British Columbia should not neglect to stock them. The wolf—the deer's worst natural enemy—does not exist in these islands, and the snowfall is light. A few deer placed in an unsettled part of the islands would rapidly increase in numbers and spread abundantly over the entire area.

A wind sprang up when we were opposite Massett, and sailing to *Delcatla* we found Captain Thompson waiting for me and in a hurry to depart.

I had some supper at *Delcatla*, and shortly after left that hospitable ranch to go aboard the *Urius* with Mr. Harrison, who was departing for a short trip to Ketchikan. The anchor up, we were propelled to Massett, where I took leave of the Indians, and soon we were on the open sea. A heavy storm arose and we were obliged to go below and endure the gasoline

fumes all night while the small schooner was tossed
about by the waves. It was a dangerous crossing and
we barely escaped being swamped. But early in the
morning we reached smoother water, and, before noon,
Ketchikan, where I endured six blank days of continual rain-storm. On November 30 the steamer *Dol-
phin* appeared, and after a three days' trip, in rainy
weather, landed me in Seattle, at which point I took
the train and reached New York, December 9.

⋅   ⋅   ⋅   ⋅   ⋅   ⋅   ⋅   ⋅

Two years after my trip to Virago Sound a new city
had been located in Massett Inlet on part of the ground
formerly occupied by *Delcatla*. The quiet peace pervading the waters and woods had been broken by the
hiss of steam and the buzz of the saw-mill. The maj-
esty of the great primitive forest had been invaded.
Blows of the axe, the noise of the handsaw, and the
crash of fallen trees sounding from its austere depths
were announcing its doom. The turmoil of industry
had begun, and white settlers had appeared to divert
the Indians from their primitive life.

November 1, 1908, Matthew Yeomans and Henry
White, two half-breeds, were hunting in a large swamp-
barren three or four miles inland, midway between
the mouth of the Naden River and Kung—one of the
barrens south of my camp and through which I had
tramped several times. Near the centre of the barren
they saw four caribou—two bulls with horns, a cow,
and a calf. The animals seemed to have no fear of
man, for they stood quite still until one after another,

except the calf, were shot down. The skins and skulls were sent to the Provincial Museum in Victoria, where I inspected them in the fall of 1909 as they were about to be mounted.*

Mr. Harrison, who communicated to me the above facts, has advised me in a letter, dated August 1, 1910, that no caribou have since been seen. After the killing the British Columbia authorities immediately placed the caribou of the Queen Charlotte Islands under the protection of the law and prohibited the shooting of any more of them.

So far as known at present, therefore, the caribou ranges in Graham Island north of latitude 54°.

.   .   .   .

The skins received by the Provincial Museum in Victoria were so poorly prepared for mounting that the energetic director, Francis Kermode, made a special trip to the caribou district near Naden Harbor, in October, 1910, for the purpose of securing some better specimens of the animals.

He was unsuccessful. First, he hunted about the barrens where the caribou had been killed. Although he recovered the old bones of the slain animals, he saw only the old tracks of two caribou heading north. Having among his guides one of the men who had been with me, he then went with him to my old camp and made a thorough search in that section, but did not find even a single track in the locality.

In answer to my letter, suggesting that the caribou

* See Appendix B, giving a description of these specimens.

will soon be extinct, he writes, January 11, 1911: "I
have made a great many inquiries from men that have
prospected that country through to the west coast,
and none of them have ever seen the caribou, but have
seen only a track here and there; in fact, the three
specimens that I have here are the only ones that I
could say were killed in that country, and I believe
myself, after having been over the country, that the
species is almost extinct. If it is not, more tracks
would have been seen, now that the Queen Charlotte
Islands are opening up."

A Salmon Creek on Admiralty Island

1 I sailed
. iree days
but two
aska, had
which to
on. It
but to
ll one of
mp, nor
The
moon,
A
the

noon on the
beam, with good
the bow, and a small
was owned by Messrs.
Juneau, who accompanied

..... Creek on ' ...... of 'y Island

CHAPTER XI

ADMIRALTY ISLAND

On September 10, 1909, Mrs. Sheldon and I sailed from Seattle on the steamer *Jefferson*, and three days later landed at Juneau. Since we could spare but two months for an outing, Admiralty Island, in Alaska, had been selected as the most accessible place in which to hunt the large bears of the southeast-coast region. It was not my purpose to do any of the shooting, but to make an opportunity for my companion to kill one of the bears. She had never before been in camp, nor had she fired a rifle more than a few times. The familiar rain-storm hailed our arrival in the afternoon, but it did not prevent plans being made at once. A small gasoline launch was hired to bring us to the south end of the island, and Bill Williams, an old prospector, was employed to assist us in camp. The following day provisions and a camp outfit were purchased, and we were ready to make the start as soon as the storm subsided sufficiently for safe navigation in a small boat.

September 16.—Although it continued to rain equally hard the next day, we departed just before noon on the *Iowa*, a small launch of forty feet beam, with good gasoline power, a pilot-house in the bow, and a small cabin for sleeping. The boat was owned by Messrs. Dickinson and Hunter, of Juneau, who accompanied

171

us as pilot and engineer. Williams brought his small gasoline boat, practically a dory, in which a light gasoline engine had been installed. We had two tents and small stoves, the provisions commonly used by Alaska prospectors, and plenty of clothing.

Although mist obscured the mountains, we sailed along Douglas Island through fairly calm water, but opposite the Taku arm of Frederick Sound it became so rough that we were obliged to go into Oliver Inlet, on the north end of Admiralty Island, to wait for better weather. There were still two hours of daylight, and while Dickinson went over a trail to the head of Seymour Canal to hunt ducks, Mrs. Sheldon and I walked down the beach in the hope of seeing a deer. After waiting and watching, without success, until dark, we returned to the boat and were soon joined by Dickinson, who had shot three fine mallards. Crowding into the little cabin about eight feet square, five of us stowed ourselves both in bunks and in canvas suspended from the roof and passed the night.

September 17.—At daylight we started again, and the boat was forced against wind and tide in a heavy sea, while the rain poured down. The mountains of Admiralty Island were covered with fog, but the shore was visible, and after coasting along near it we entered Pybus Bay and, at 2.30 P. M., dropped anchor in a small bight on the west side, about four miles from the entrance. We had watched the shore during the whole trip and only one deer had been seen—a doe, which trotted off untouched, after Dickinson had fired at her five or six times. The feature of the trip was the great quantities of scoters, assembled in large flocks in the water and close to the shore.

Just after anchoring, the clouds lifted, and Williams and I went on shore to select a spot on which temporarily to erect the tent until a better situation could be found. After an hour had been spent in putting it up, the storm again descended with so much wind and rain that it was doubtful if the tent would stand in such an exposed place. Taking a skiff, I rowed along the beach and found a more sheltered spot at the edge of the woods. The provisions were landed and placed under a tree, a canvas covering was thrown over them, and we had an hour before dark in which to erect the tent over a wet and muddy surface. It was soon put up; boughs were cut and thrown on the ground; the stove was set up and a fire started. Mrs. Sheldon, who was having her first introduction to "rough camp," had wisely selected sufficient food from the provision supply and brought it to the tent. Over mud and water, under leaking canvas, in a space seven feet square, we slept on the boughs while the heavy rain beat through the old canvas and dripped upon us all night. The boat had started back, but finding the sea too rough outside, Dickinson anchored her in the bight, where she remained until she left early the next morning.

September 18.—The storm continued all the next day. After finding more suitable ground for a permanent camp, Williams and I began to cut poles and were hard at work with our axes when Mrs. Sheldon called my attention to some animals near the opposite shore.

I looked across and saw three bears pottering about close to the water.

In a moment our two rifles were taken out of the cases and we started to walk a mile around the beach, or rather a rocky shore covered with slippery sea-weeds, which constantly kept popping as we trod upon them. Finally we approached the curve of the beach and, advancing cautiously, I looked ahead, but the bears were not there. We circled around into another bight and soon found ourselves on some vast tide flats, over which we wandered for some time without seeing the animals again. I noticed several places where they had been digging out the roots of the wild parsnip, which grows close to the shore in clear spaces on the edge of the tide flats, but the woods being near, the bears had evidently entered them. We returned in time for lunch, and the afternoon was spent in felling trees, clearing the ground, and getting ready to make the camp.

September 19.—In rain and fog we worked all the next day, cutting and notching big logs which were framed up four high, and nailing on poles over which the tent could be thrown. All the afternoon was spent in cutting a supply of firewood. During the continual rains in the fall, scarcity of fuel wood is really an obstacle to convenient camping on Admiralty Island. All drift-wood on the shore, as well as nearly all standing timber, is water-soaked. None of the fallen dead logs will burn, and the only resource is to find dead yellow cedars which are scarce near the shore. A few were standing on the slope of a steep ridge several hundred

yards above our camp, and, after chopping them, we had
to shoulder the logs and worry through dense woods to
the camp, where they could be sawed and split into
lengths suitable for the stoves. Green alder wood
mixed with the dry cedar burns well after the fire is
started, and an abundant supply was near the camp.

September 20.—We crowded into the leaky tent for the
last time that night, and the next morning commenced
· to construct a bunk at the end of the log frame. Directly in front of camp were two small ponds fed by
a clear brook which dashed down the slope, and I was
surprised to see a water-ouzel sitting on a rock which
rose in the centre of one of the ponds. It was not in
the least timid, but allowed me to approach closely and
watch it. After watching the water for a moment it
would suddenly dive and emerge with a white worm
in its mouth, which was quickly swallowed. Then
jumping to another rock in the same manner it would
dive for another worm. Many times during my stay
in that camp the water-ouzel returned to the pond to
feed.

At eleven in the morning, when Mrs. Sheldon and
I were placing boughs on the bunk, Williams, who was
standing on the beach, beckoned to me and pointed
across the bight. Looking over I saw the three bears
feeding in about the same place where we had seen
them before. Mrs. Sheldon and I immediately started.
The tide, being high, covered the smoother part of the
beach, and we were obliged to pick our way over a
jumble of rocks which covered the steep slope to the
water. Some time was therefore required to reach a

point near where the bears were feeding, and we must also approach them with the utmost caution. I kept close to the woods, expecting to meet the bears at each curve on the shore. Finally it became necessary to climb around a rocky ledge sloping so steeply to the deep and surging water that our foothold was retained with difficulty. On the other side was a little baylet only twenty-five yards in width and indenting the shore for about the same distance. At its head was a grassy space extending for a few yards between the woods and the water. A hundred yards farther along the shore, round another curve, was the spot where the bears had been seen feeding when we started.

Though it was raining heavily, there was not a breath of wind. Followed closely by Mrs. Sheldon, I slowly and cautiously crept around the point of the ledge and saw a bear silently stepping out of the woods toward the small grass plot, followed by two others. They proceeded in single file close to overhanging alders, but somewhat obscured by the high grass, they were inconspicuous. In a moment they would reach the open and head directly toward us. Realizing that Mrs. Sheldon was not accustomed to shooting a rifle, and that her aim might not be certain when three bears were approaching not fifty yards away, I knew it was best that she should wait until her game stood out clearly against the background. She had chosen a sitting position so that she could sight the rifle, and acknowledged with composure my whispered questions and directions as the bears silently glided along at a leisurely pace, quite unconscious of us, while their huge bulks looked formidable indeed as they approached. Glancing at Mrs. Sheldon, I saw that she was perfectly cool; the rifle was at her shoulder, and she was looking over the sight, apparently keeping it on the moving bear. As it stepped out into the open and faced in our direction, and while I was expecting the shot, a breeze suddenly eddied around the point from behind, blowing directly toward the bears. I saw the first one toss its head, sniffing. I whispered: "Shoot quickly; they will run!" and simultaneously the two in the rear faced about, disappearing with a bound into the woods, while, a second later, the leader turned with a spring, and another jump put it out of sight just as Mrs. Sheldon fired. I heard her exclamation of disappointment. That gust of wind and her bad luck had defeated us. The second bear being the one first seen by her, she had covered it with her rifle and followed it so intently that the leader had escaped her notice until it was disappearing, when she swung the rifle and shot at it.

I hurried over into the woods, but there was no blood sign. The game, this time, had escaped. During the trip to Alaska and in Juneau everybody had impressed Mrs. Sheldon with the ferocity and aggressiveness of the Admiralty Island bears, and it was, therefore, encouraging for our future chances to see that she had remained perfectly cool, even more so than most men would have done when three bears were approaching so closely. Since I did not care to leave our tracks about the country more than necessary, we did not attempt to follow. Coming over in his boat, Williams

brought us back to camp, and by the late afternoon the
tent was transferred over the frame, the stove put in, a
table constructed, abundant firewood split, and everything was arranged comfortably for a long stay. Williams's tent was erected on dry ground also, and conveniently arranged for him.

It was the mystic hour of evening when our work
was finished, and, the clouds having lifted, the rain
suddenly stopped. It was calm, and a peaceful silence brooded over woods and waters. Mrs. Sheldon
and I walked far out on a point of reefs. Everywhere
ducks were lazily floating on the surface of the water, which reflected the large trees towering near the
shores as well as the high, snow-crested mountains
behind them. Huge reefs were scattered all about,
snow-white with the thousands of gulls which flocked
on them to pass the night. Little islands, covered by
groves of lofty trees, were numerous, and on one of
these, in the top of a gigantic dead spruce, a fine bald
eagle and its mate now perched facing each other, each
one calling at short intervals in a series of shrill screams
which echoed about the irregular shores. A wonderful
yellow-golden sky overspread the mountain summits
at the head of the basin, clouds rich in sunset colors
were banked in patches, and the waters reflected a
glory of light and color which harmonized with the
beautiful landscape surrounding us. Mists were rising from the woods, here and there even creeping up
the tree-clad slopes of the ridges and mountains, while
to the east all was leaden gray except the tops of the
ridges, which were touched with light.

Our camp in Pybus Bay.

View up the bight from camp

Admiralty Island is about ninety miles long and
varies in width from thirty to forty miles, except at
the north end above Hawk Inlet, where it is very narrow. Like all the Alaska coast islands, its topography
has been chiselled by glaciers, its mountains extending

Map of Admiralty and Adjacent Islands.

north and south in parallel ranges through the centre.
High and rough, many of them throw out spurs, some
of which, enclosing large basins, reach almost to the
shore. Some of the crests of the higher mountains hold
perennial snow, and below the crests of others small
dying glaciers still remain. Irregular ridges, precipitous like the mountains, extend in all directions, only
dying out at the coast. Vast areas are rolling swamp,
with yellow cedars, mostly dead, and bull pines scat-

tered over the surface. Although there is a liberal
supply of undergrowth in the swamps, they are fairly
open as compared with the timbered country, but
different in character from the swamp-barrens of the
Queen Charlotte Islands, which are practically entirely
open.

The surface of the country is as rough and densely
covered with brush and windfalls as that of the other
coast islands and the adjacent main-land. Sallal does
not exist there, but huckleberry (*Vaccinium*) grows so
dense that it forms almost as much of an obstacle to
tramping about as the sallal does on Graham Island.
Devil's-club also is exceedingly dense near the rivers and
creeks as high up as there is any volume of water; in
places salmon-berry grows on the slopes, so that, on the
whole, progress in walking is the same toilsome con-
flict with nature as elsewhere on other islands along
the southern coasts of Alaska and British Columbia.
Vast parks of gigantic trees, hemlocks and spruces,
with moss-carpeted surface fairly free from undergrowth, occur scattered through the island and remind
one of the big forests of Vancouver Island.

There is found on Admiralty Island the usual bird
life* of the other coast islands; and the mammal life
is also quite similar to that of adjacent reigons, with
the exception of new varieties of bear, beaver, *Castor
canadensis phæus;* mink, *Lutreola vison nesolestes*, and
a field-mouse, *Microtus admiraltiæ*. Deer, *Odocoileus*

---

* Those interested should see "Birds and Mammals of the 1907
Alexander Expedition to Southeastern Alaska." Separate from vol.
5, University of California Publications in Zoology, 1909.

By permission of U. S. Biological Survey.

Photograph by W. H. Osgood.

columbianus sitkensis, are very abundant all over the island. The otter, *Lutra canadensis periclyzomæ* (?), abounds everywhere; the beaver exists in some places in the interior, and high on the mountains marmots are found. Weasels, mice, shrews, and bats comprise the rest of the mammal life. Wolves, foxes, rabbits, and red squirrels do not exist there. The bear, a variety of the Alaska brown bears of the coast, somewhat smaller than some of the northern varieties, has been described by Dr. Merriam as a separate species, *Ursus eulophus*. A closely related species, *Ursus sitkensis*, exists on the three neighboring islands, to the west— Baranof, Chichagof, and Kruzof. Admiralty, these two large islands, and Kruzof, are the only ones on which the brown coast bears of Alaska exist, south of Montague Island. Black bears, common on all other islands of sufficient size south of Admiralty, do not exist on the four which contain brown bears.

Pybus Bay, about eight miles long and from two to three miles wide, has rock-bound shores and is filled with reefs. The lofty mountains are on the west and send out spurs to form two magnificent basins about three miles apart, near the lower end of the bay. We were camped near the upper one. High mountains surround the head of the bay, but they are several miles distant from the shore. On the east side are high ridges all covered with timber. Salmon rivers, flowing from the basins, enter bights, and one enters the head of the bay also. There is said to be a small salmon creek entering on the west side.

It was our purpose to hunt the bears as they came

into the rivers for salmon, both in the two basins and at the head of the bay. The mountains surrounding the basin in front of our camp were high and impressive, with rugged outlines; the valley formed between them was densely timbered, broken into ridges and flats on either side of the rivers, which descended in a racing torrent from the snows, five miles distant, at the head of the basin. All the mountains are similar to those of Montague Island, and the slopes of the ridges are as precipitous—in fact, they are mostly like vast ledges covered with timber.

CHAPTER XII

EXPERIENCES WITH BEARS NEAR THE SALMON RIVERS

September 21.—It continued to rain very hard all the next day, but, putting on rubber boots and slickers, we started out to learn the lay of the country and if possible to provide a supply of meat for the camp by killing a deer. In the far-away country of Alaska, in places where game is as abundant as in Admiralty Island, the first task necessary is to secure a supply of fresh meat. When seeking special game difficult to find and kill, like bears, time spent in killing deer may be at the expense of success in the other pursuit, and the first deer seen—whether doe, fawn, or buck—is killed, if possible, so that, with the meat supply secure, no more valuable time need be consumed in hunting for it.

For the first time in my experience in the humid coast country of the Northwest, I was clad in a costume fairly water-proof—and that was only practicable since we intended to keep out of the woods as much as possible—rubber boots and slicker. We walked half a mile around the beach to the head of the bight and crossed the strip of narrow land extending out nearly a mile between it and a larger bight into which the rivers of the basin entered.

In the centre of this strip, near the head of the bight, was a pretty little lake of half an acre, nestled in the woods, where we saw a few white-cheeked geese and some gadwall ducks, all of which were quickly frightened away. Bear tracks, some of them quite fresh, were about, and numerous diggings for the root of the wild parsnip were seen over the grassy spots where it grew. Passing through an open lane connecting the two bights, we reached the second one at low tide.

The sight before us was one especially characteristic of those island flats at that season, yet it was invested with sufficient individual charm to make it linger long in the memory. Vast mud flats and grassy marsh meadows, interspersed with acres of shallow water and little islands covered with gigantic hemlock trees rising abruptly from the level, stretched out before us. Thousands of ducks—mallards, pintail, gadwall, teal, and wild geese—were in the water. The air was full of screaming gulls, particularly along the creeks; great flocks of geese were feeding on the flats; ravens were numerous everywhere; and large numbers of bald eagles were standing on the ground and flying around, while numerous flocks of sandpipers and shore birds added to the active bird life.

Half a mile west, along these flats, we came to the salmon creeks—one quite small, rising not far back on the south side of the basin, the other much larger, discharging a good volume of water through a width of from fifty to a hundred feet, and full of deep pools and swift riffles. The water was clear as crystal and icy cold. Going to the smaller creek, where large flocks of gulls, numerous ravens, and bald eagles were congregated, we crossed it and entered the woods, or

rather the devil's-club thickets which extend for varying distances back. Well-beaten bear trails leading
to the creek were all along the banks, and fresh remains of eaten salmon were everywhere.

Taking a short circuit, we reached the larger creek
and crossed near a curve where bear signs were
numerous and the woods were fairly clear on the
north side. Entering these, we climbed; a low hill,
from the top of which we could look below through
the big hemlocks and see the river. The creek,
gliding and dancing over its rocky bars, under great
overhanging trees, presented a lively scene in that
dense wilderness. Salmon were splashing and fighting in all the pools and wriggling up the shallow
riffles. Honking geese kept flying up and down;
large flocks of gulls were busy in continual flight
along the creek; mallard ducks floated down, followed
shortly by red-breasted mergansers, and later by a
great blue heron, squawking as it soared along. The
woods were silent, and the whole picture of forest life
during the run of salmon was below us. Yet, not all
of the forest life, for the big bear did not appear.

After resting a while, we continued through the
woods to the mouth of the larger creek, and at low tide
went to the head of the larger bight, where I succeeded in finding enough dry wood to make a fire so
that tea could be brewed. Two bears had recently
crossed the mud flats. In the woods I had observed
the stellar jay, winter-wrens, and the dwarf hermit-
thrush. In the pass near the flats were great numbers
of sparrows, and now and then we flushed jacksnipes.

We reached camp late in the afternoon, but, as an hour remained before dark, I went down the beach in the hope of shooting a deer; I returned, however, without having seen anything but a track or two which indicated that one had come out from the woods, travelled a few yards in the open, and returned to cover.

September 22.—The next day a heavy southeast storm descended so violently that we gave up bear-hunting and went down along the beach for deer. Travelling several hours among the rocks and often penetrating the woods, we saw nothing but occasional tracks. It is difficult to walk along the beach of Pybus Bay, since the shore slopes abruptly over rough bar-nacled rocks, all of which are covered with slippery sea-weed. Numerous log-jams have to be crossed, and in places ledges fall directly into deep water. Only in small baylets, and occasionally in other places, is there a smoother stretch, and then only for a few feet. The tide rises from nine to fourteen feet, and at high tide one must keep mostly in the woods, which are very dense near the shore.

After we had taken some lunch in camp, I looked across the bight and was surprised to see the three bears again feeding in the same place. The tide was high and Williams tried to row us across, but as the fierce squalls and driving rain made it impossible to keep a course, we landed well up the bight. On arriving at the place we found that the bears had disappeared. We spent some time looking for them, both on the beach and in the adjacent woods, but never saw them again.

Wading the salmon creek.   September 21.

View up the bight from camp in Pybus Bay.

The sun had not appeared for ten days. Nothing but rain, wind, and storm, except for the few hours with one clear evening sky!

September 23.—There was no wind in the morning, but all day it was dark and gloomy, while the rain fell steadily in a downpour heavier than any we had before experienced. Mist and fog filled the woods so that it was not practicable to watch the salmon creeks with any chance of success. Nevertheless, we crossed to the flats and watched for several hours, but it was not possible to see more than a short distance, and we returned in the afternoon. While standing in the open, it was startling to hear the creeks booming in the woods like the roar of a heavy wind blowing through the trees, while the water-falls, dashing down the mountain slopes, added a more distant and awe-inspiring sound.

September 24.—There was a steady downpour all the next day, but the fog had lifted sufficiently to make hunting possible. We waited until the tide was low, and then, crossing the flats, attempted to wade the smaller creek in order to gain a favorable position for watching, but the stream was running a flood and could not be crossed. Soon as the wind increased and mists began to settle, we entered a small park of big hemlock-trees to wait for better weather. But the storm constantly increased and the dark woods afforded little protection from the rain falling both from and through the branches of the trees.

The roar of rushing waters sounding on all sides added a sense of wild desolation to the impressions conveyed by the darkening gloom of the forest, and we were about to start for camp when Mrs. Sheldon, who was facing the woods, suddenly picked up her rifle and whispered that deer were approaching. Looking in that direction, I saw a fawn followed by a doe, with another fawn bringing up the rear—all walking rapidly with agile steps, and in line to pass about fifty yards in front of us. Mrs. Sheldon quickly fired at the leading fawn, which ran forward a few steps and fell as the doe turned back into the woods. But a few seconds later, Mrs. Sheldon, watching her opportunity as the animal passed between the trees, shot it through the heart. Hurrying to the fawn, I quickly dressed it and then went to the doe, which had fallen in its tracks. After gralloching it and cutting some strips of the skin for thongs, I placed the fawn inside and lashed the opening together; then, taking them on my shoulders, while both rifles were carried by Mrs. Sheldon, we started for camp. While I was dressing the doe the second fawn came walking almost directly up to us, but, getting our scent, turned and ran off into the woods. The stomach of the doe contained a variety of leaves and was full of huckleberries. Its udder was still full of milk. The fawn's stomach contained also leaves and berries, a gratifying fact to us, as it showed that the other one was old enough to take care of itself.

The tide was getting so high that it required some time to bring the carcasses to camp. At last we had a good supply of meat and could devote our time wholly to the hunting of bears.

Meat obtained.   September 24.

Photograph by W. H. Osgood.   By permission of U. S. Biological Survey.
Moss-draped spruce.   Admiralty Island.

September 25.—The rain stopped that night, and the next day was one of heavy showers, between intervals of wind. We never tried to go around to the creeks until the tide was fairly low, since, when the flats were covered, a long détour through the woods was necessary to reach them. This was not only difficult but unwise, because no bear that might approach would cross our trail without running off. At low tide, therefore, we went to the creek, which, like all the creeks of the Alaska coast, rapidly subsided after a storm, and we found that by fording it we could reach an advantageous position to watch for bears. The flood produced by the recent storms had washed thousands of weak salmon out to the salt-water, and all the gulls, eagles, and ravens of the region seemed to be congregated near the mouth of the small creek. Several large flocks of migrating robins were seen, and once or twice, as the sun threatened to break through the clouds, varied thrushes welcomed it with their sweet, golden song, somewhat reduced in volume as compared with that of spring, but adding an indescribable charm to the woods.

The head and entrails of the doe had disappeared, but those of the fawn had not been touched.

The point I had selected for watching was on a bank exactly where the creek curves to form a right angle, favorable for seeing a hundred yards in either of two directions. Behind us was a forest of huge hemlocks and spruces, the surface covered with a growth of huckleberry bushes so dense as to obstruct the vision in any direction except for a few feet. Across the creek was a narrow meadow bordering the woods and continuing to the open flats beyond. On the left, the creek was fringed with dense devil's-club and alder. Every ten or twenty feet along the bank were well-beaten bear trails leading out from the woods on both sides, and one was directly behind us. Fresh bear tracks were everywhere; and the numerous fresh remains of salmon scattered all about demonstrated that bears were feeding there every afternoon or night. We remained quietly watching until the rising tide warned us to leave.

Although no bear approached, our interest was aroused and sustained by the sight before us on the salmon creek. Below was a swift, shallow riffle falling from a deep pool just above it. Every few moments a large dog-salmon or a humpback-salmon would attempt to wriggle up, sometimes with success, sometimes without. All were weakened salmon which had before been up the creek but had been washed out by the storm and were then trying to go up again. The pool was filled with spawning salmon, which kept up a continual splashing as they dug out hollows in the shallow parts by pushing down the head and whipping the water with the tail. Each male was guarding its mate and fighting off any other salmon that might approach its bed where the female was depositing eggs. Bruised and battered, those salmon displayed in unceasing activity their wonderful vitality during the frenzy of race propagation. Once I saw a dog-salmon try to ascend a riffle which descended in a small channel not two inches deep. It wriggled in rapid, snakelike motions almost completely out of water for five or more minutes, until it actually climbed over the riffle to the deeper water above. There it was immediately attacked by two others which were guarding their own spawning-beds.

Still more interesting were the flocks of short-billed gulls—including several hundred of them—which kept flying again and again to the pool, alighting in the spawning-beds in shallow water and diving quickly and repeatedly for the eggs. They cleaned up the eggs within reach, where the water was shallow enough, and then flew a short distance up or down the creek to another pool. After an interval, when the salmon had deposited fresh eggs, they would reappear to pick them up. These gulls, together with several varieties of ducks, must eat nearly all the eggs deposited in shallow water. The larger gulls—herring and glaucus-winged gulls—only seem to feed on the dead salmon, as do also the ravens, crows, and eagles. When the creek was at a flood, in the heavy rains, I observed thousands of short-billed gulls flying above the current lower down, near low-tide level. All were continually dipping in the current to gather the floating eggs which were being forced out by the swifter flow.

Not only must the noble salmon die after entering its river to spawn, but countless millions of its eggs are consumed by gulls and ducks. I had noted the absence of gulls following the steamer in early September, and did not then know that nearly all were busy securing their food in the salmon streams.

We also saw a fine mink running along the bank and

occasionally diving into the water. There is an indescribable grace and ease about the motion of a mink
as it glides along, silently and mysteriously, without
appearing to be impeded in the least by the numerous
obstacles to its progress along the irregular bank.

September 26–27.—It was rainy rather than stormy
the next two days, during which Mrs. Sheldon took a
much-needed rest and remained about camp, while I
busied myself making corduroy paths near the tent
where the ground had become soft mud. Once or
twice the sun was faintly visible through the mists,
and it was clear again on the evening of September
27, when we went out on the reef to enjoy the perfect calm, the sight of the water-fowl, and that of the
two eagles which regularly repaired to that same dead
tree to pass the night. Besides the wonderful evening
sky, a brilliant rainbow formed its arc over the bay,
only becoming faint where the light tipped the tops
of the ridges on the other side.

September 28.—September 28 was very warm, but
a heavy rain fell all day. We could not go to the creek
in the morning when the tide was high, but arrived at
our watching-place shortly before three in the afternoon and took our positions. Numerous fresh remains
of salmon showed that bears were still regularly feeding there, and, seated on each side of a big tree close to
the bank, we maintained the watch, while the salmon
were splashing and fighting among the gulls, which were
hopping about as they dived for their eggs. There
was no wind, no noise except the murmur of the creek,
the screaming of the gulls, and the patter of the rain.

All the conditions were favorable for a bear to approach, and, constantly alert, with straining eyes and ears, we silently waited for two hours. It began to grow perceptibly darker, and our eagerness was then intense as we carefully watched the numerous openings in the brush which had been made by the bears in their repeated trips to the creek for salmon. The growth was so dense that it was not possible to see a bear before it emerged from the brush on the edge of the bank.

We were seated about three feet apart, in front of a large spruce-tree, with rifles across our knees, when Mrs. Sheldon, turning her head to the left, discovered a large male bear standing motionless in the alders exactly *six feet* away, with ears cocked forward, intently watching her. Not a sound or suspicion of its noiseless approach had we received. As she now lifted her rifle, she turned and whispered to me, but the motion was fatal to her chance of a shot, for the next moment a great crash in the brush told its own story. The bear, instead of chancing upon one of the numerous trails at short distances above and below us, had taken one which reached the creek three feet to our left, and, seeing Mrs. Sheldon, had stopped to watch the unusual apparition. Her quick motion, as she turned to me, frightened it, and with a sudden jump backward it disappeared in the brush. Seeing the huckleberry bushes moving about forty feet up on an incline, I pointed my rifle and fired. A great thrashing about in the brush was quickly succeeded by sounds indicating the bear's rapid retreat.

I hurried forward and soon found blood, then some pieces of entrails and some stomach contents. Shortly the trail led to an open glade, where the tracks showed that the bear had been running with long bounds until it reached the dense woods filled with alder growing on a swampy surface. Here the trail was lost, and a hundred yards beyond was the side of the mountain. As soon as I had seen the positive evidence of a stomach shot, I knew that the bear would escape.

It was almost dark, and, returning, I found Mrs. Sheldon somewhat nervous for my safety, but we both went into the woods again to continue the hopeless search until the darkness drove us to camp. The track of the bear was that of a mature male, and back in the trail by which it had approached I noticed that it had been digging skunk cabbage. That night a high wind blew from the west, and for the first time the stars were visible.

September 29.—Wednesday, September 29, was the first day we passed without rain, nor did clouds gather until the afternoon. During the high tide of the morning we pushed through the woods to the head of the bight where the meadow-grass was white with the frost that had fallen during the night. Reaching the woods where I had lost the trail of the wounded bear, we made a thorough search for footprints but could not discover a sign of one. In the bright sunshine the wilderness seemed cheerful indeed after the dark, stormy days that had gone before. The white mountain crests were clear, and the woods were silent and inviting, while great shadows were cast upon the green

moss, among the exquisite ferns scattered in thousands
on the surface of the ground, and even well up on the
trunks of the huge fir-trees.

Crossing to the flat in order to avoid the arduous
work of fighting back through the woods, we found the
· tide again rising rapidly and were soon surrounded with
water flowing swiftly on all sides of us.   To reach the
woods we were obliged to wade up to our hips in a
sweep of tide so strong that Mrs. Sheldon was nearly
carried off her feet.

After lunch we entered the boat and went to the
bight three miles below.   Two salmon creeks, a large
one and a small one, entered at the head, both meet-
ing the salt-water about a hundred yards apart.   At
low tide large flats are exposed, and as we approached
the numerous gulls, ravens, eagles, and crows flying
about the mouth of the creeks indicated that salmon
were there.   The mountains beyond, enclosing a narrow, deep basin which extends three or four miles inland, are higher, more rugged, and more impressive
than those in the basin beyond our camp.   A large
dead glacier lies under the crest of one on the south
side, and the slopes of all are so precipitous that numerous cascades, falling from the tops, leap over precipices and dash through the timber in such a way that
they appear like continuous white stripes down the
mountain-sides.

At the foot of that magnificent basin we took our
seats and waited, while Williams took his boat two
miles out, near the entrance to the bight.   There was
no favorable position from which to watch either creek,

since the alders were so dense that the field of vision
was obstructed except for a short distance. Bear signs
were as numerous as in the other salmon creeks, but
the wind was blowing up and no bear approached.
After making a short reconnoissance in the woods until
dusk, we waded out to meet the returning boat and
then returned to camp. It was clear to me that our
best chance for bears was along the creeks nearer camp,
and in the morning as the tide began to fall we started.

September 30.—A light rain was falling, but after the
good weather we did not anticipate a storm. We followed the woods on the north side of the larger creek,
and struggled through the underbrush until we were a
mile and a half up the creek where we could wade.
Slowly passing up the riffles, climbing over fallen logs,
and walking on the banks around the deep pools, we
gradually penetrated some distance into the centre
of the woods.

The creek was full of herring gulls and mallard
ducks—all eating the dead salmon, which were rotting
on the banks and in the slack water of the pools. Numerous remains of half-eaten salmon scattered about
near the bear trails leading, at least every hundred feet,
to the river, demonstrated the activity of the bears
when seeking their main food during the salmon season. I noticed that before eating them they had
usually brought the salmon from the river to the bank,
often many yards back, and sometimes to the tops of
hills situated near the river. But it was discouraging
to see no live salmon in the creek, not even in those
parts where there had been thousands the first day

Mountains bordering the lower bight.

that we had ascended but a short distance. At length
I determined to cross through the thicket of devil's-
club and alders a full mile to the smaller creek, where
possibly the salmon might still be spawning.

Few who have not experienced the difficulty of fighting through those vast swamps bordering the rivers
of Admiralty Island can realize what it means. The
whole flat, always flooded at high water, is intersected
by numerous deep, narrow channels which can be
crossed only by walking over small fallen logs. The
whole surface is boggy, windfalls are abundant, and big
logs have to be circumvented. Devil's-club and alders
are so dense that they are almost interwoven. Foot
by foot we had to fight our way along, until at last the
creek appeared. Not a salmon remained in it. The
last heavy storm had washed all of them out to the salt-
water, and the few that were still in the two pools at
the mouth of the small creek were those which were
strong enough to wriggle back to the first pools suitable
for spawning.

On the other side of the creek was a precipitous ridge
covered with gigantic hemlocks and spruces. The
rain had stopped, and, finding a way to ascend, we selected a spot on the edge of a precipice fairly overhanging the creek. Here we rested and ate some lunch.
The creek, seen from above, was an impressive sight
as it raced in riffles through the woods. Suddenly
we saw a flock of six mergansers floating down the
swift current, now and then pausing to dive for a stray
salmon egg, until lost to sight. That was the only
evidence of life we saw near that creek, and as the

woods were fairly close to it, we walked along a deer trail at the edge of the precipice, thereby getting a fair view below.

Descending, we again accomplished the difficult task of crossing the swamp and reached the river as the rain began to pour. After forcing through the devil's-club, it was a positive pleasure to wade with ease down the long stretches of shallow rapids. Here and there a great dead log had fallen completely across the creek in such a way that the current bored under and scooped the bottom to a depth of three or four feet on the lower side, where pools of eddying water were formed. Coming to one of these logs, it was necessary to go out on the bank and walk across on it to the other side where the water was shallow. Quickly passing along the log and stepping into the shallow water, I had started down the stream without looking back, when an exclamation and a splash caused me to turn quickly. My companion had slipped and was lying on her back in a bubbling, ice-cold pool three feet in depth, her head just above the water-line, while one hand was holding up her rifle at arm's-length. "I did not get the rifle wet, anyway!" was her consolatory comment as I helped her to her feet and then hastened forward to find a dry piece of ground on the bank where she could empty the water from her rubber boots.

We had waded fifty yards farther before another log was seen lying across the surface of the creek. I was looking to the left for a place to cross, when suddenly Mrs. Sheldon, who was slightly behind, on my right, threw up her rifle and fired, and I saw a large bear disappear in the thick devil's-club on the right bank fifty feet ahead. It had stood motionless, partially concealed, watching our approach. She saw it just before it turned to run and, remembering her last experience, took the only chance—a snap-shot—but missed, as nearly any one else would have done under the same circumstances. I could find no blood sign, and continuing to wade until the water was too deep, crossed through the woods to the creek's mouth.

Although a severe southeast storm had developed, going to the mouth of the smaller creek, we watched for two hours, until the storm increased to such an extent that we were obliged to return to camp.

CHAPTER XIII

HUNTING THE ADMIRALTY ISLAND BEAR

THE wind blew a hurricane that night, causing the tent, which was protected by an ill-fitting fly, to leak in places.

October 1.—At dawn the sky had cleared, the air was crisp, and except for a few showers at midday, the weather was all that could be desired. As we approached the flats, a doe was seen crossing the head of the bight, first wading through the shallow water until the deep channel was reached, when it leaped across and continued around the shore in our direction. When it had approached within one hundred and fifty feet I photographed it. We then continued to the head of the little lake, where I attempted to photograph the seven geese that were usually feeding there in the early morning. Creeping forward in the brush, I was almost within range when one lifted its head and began to honk as a warning. Immediately all looked toward me and sprang up in flight.

Crossing to the flats, fewer eagles were observed, but the mallards, widgeons, teals, ravens, crows, and geese were as abundant as usual, but only the larger gulls were there in numbers. We took a position on a small elevated island near the centre of the flats, for the purpose of watching the open country. About noon, as

200

"When it approached to within one hundred and fifty yards I photographed it."   October 1.

I was looking over the mountains through my field-glasses, a bear was seen feeding in the green grass, in a saddle connecting the two high peaks southwest of camp. It was digging out mice and eating the grass. After half an hour, it lay down, and soon another came over the crest to feed for a while in the same place and finally disappear in the trees lower down on the slope. At the same time a buck deer was visible a quarter of a mile to the right, feeding in one of the clear spaces among the timber, high on the slopes of the same mountain. It was too late to attempt to climb for the bears, and besides, the mountain slopes were so precipitous, that some reconnaissance was necessary to find a route to the top; we therefore contented ourselves, waiting and watching, until the tide should retreat low enough to permit us to walk over to the creek.

The woods seemed alive with varied thrushes, their weak notes sounding in all directions and strikingly different from their wonderful song when it is in full volume, in the spring-time. Great flocks of migrating birds were passing overhead, and the eagles were soaring about the mountain crests.

A spirited mink running along the bank greeted us as, later, we reached the creek, to find only about a dozen dog-salmon remaining in the pools. No bear appeared, and reaching camp at dark, we beheld the glory of the full moon set in the sky directly above the snowy crests at the head of the basin. Its pale light was cast over the mountain; silvery streams glinted along the water of the bight and bathed the woods in their mysterious charm. The occasional quack of a duck and honk of a goose seemed to betoken their delight also in the calm of that beautiful night.

October 2.—From sunshine and bright moonlight to storm—a heavy southeast storm, with all the elements let loose—that was what greeted our rising hopes for a continuance of better weather. The rain began early in the morning and continued all day. But we faced it and went over to the flats. Innumerable ducks, geese, and crows had concentrated there for shelter. Even a few varied thrushes sang out from the tree-tops their memory of the bright day before. Going to the creek, I realized the significance of the vanished salmon. The heavy storms had washed them out and the bears had gone to the higher country for food!

Up to that time fresh bear dung was everywhere near the creek. It had contained huckleberries, skunk-cabbage root, and salmon, including the bones. The black bears on Vancouver Island do not eat the salmon bone. I had also seen old dung containing deers' hair, but believe that it did not signify that the bears hunted deer. Deer are constantly wounded around the shores of Pybus Bay, and bears must find the carcasses of those that die. I obtained credible information from a prospector, that he had earlier in the summer seen a deer and two bears feeding on the top of a mountain within fifty feet of each other, and the deer was indifferent. Nearly all the fresh dung that I had seen contained tape-worm still alive. That day, for the first time, I saw some fresh dung composed only of grass. I knew that in the future the

only chance of killing a bear below the mountain slopes
would rest upon my seeing one straying about the flats
for dead salmon, which they eat after the live ones are
gone.

The run of the humpback and dog salmon varies,
and that year it was very early. The salmon were all
in the creeks, and very weak, when we arrived, and
it was our bad luck that the heavy storms had come
so soon. Salmon had appeared to be more plentiful
in the creeks of the lower bight, and I planned to go
down there the next day. As we were returning to
camp, a doe and two fawns were seen walking along
the beach a hundred yards ahead of us, and we watched
them until they entered the woods almost within shot
from the tent.

October 3.—While we were intermittingly progress-
ing in the boat the next morning, the rain ceased, but
the day continued cloudy. Just before reaching the
entrance of the lower bight, two does appeared a hundred yards out in the water, swimming toward shore.
They had swum a mile and a half, from the opposite
side of the bay. We ran up to within fifty feet and
they did not hasten or appear frightened until we came
in the wind, when, in a terrified state of mind, they
almost reared in the water, and putting their ears back
increased their speed. Soon touching bottom, they
fairly dashed up over the rough rocks and ran into the
woods.

As we rounded a point and could see to the head of
the bight, the numerous gulls, eagles, and ravens flying
about the creeks testified that some salmon were still

remaining in them. We landed some distance below, intending to watch in the late afternoon. While we were walking along on the north side, a fine bald eagle appeared, hopping in the grass, unable to fly, because it was so gorged with dead salmon that its crop protruded in a huge bunch, which in some way obstructed the use of its wings. As we approached, it hopped along to a point of rock where it sat while I walked to within six feet of it and photographed it.

Entering the woods and forcing through a hundred yards of brush, we reached a fine swamp-prairie, as they are locally called, and proceeded up the basin, which was soon enclosed by the rugged mountains towering close on both sides. This prairie extends from the upper bight near our camp, around to within a short distance of the head of the lower basin. It is from half a mile to a hundred yards wide and contains many large areas of clear space, filled with the little ponds so characteristic of similar country on all the Alaska islands. After going two miles, we came to two lakes of several acres each, which were filled with gadwall ducks and teals. Numerous bear trails, beaten deep into the soft ground, bore evidence of the regular habits of bears travelling from the mountain slopes to the salmon creeks; but few had loitered about the prairies.

One small creek crosses the prairies through a strip of woods two and a half miles up the basin, and there I noticed remains of coho salmon which had been eaten by a bear. The woods through which it flowed were so dense that it was not practical to watch for bears,

Bald eagle so stuffed with salmon meat that it was unable to fly.
October 3.

Mountains surrounding lower basin.   October 3.

and besides, no coho salmon were then in the creek. The cohos run up special creeks, usually those which flow from a lake, and provide the last fish food of the season for the bears, long after the other varieties of salmon cease to run. But it is not possible to watch such creeks with any degree of success, since all are small and flow through thick woods.

We had before us inspiring scenery, although we did not see any bears, even after tramping well up toward the head of the prairie. Once, as I was scanning the numerous grassy spaces on the mountain slope, all of which were likely spots for bears to feed, a buck deer appeared up near the crest. Magpies and chickadees were abundant about the edge of the prairie, and the numerous flocks of migrating birds passing overhead showed why bird life was becoming scarce.

By four o'clock we were in position, near the mouth of the smaller creek, but with little hope of seeing anything, although more than fifty salmon were in the pools. The wind was blowing directly up the creeks, and I had ascended a short distance, but found no salmon.

At dark we boarded the boat which Williams had brought back for us, and in spite of the balking engine, which could barely propel us through some heavy tide rips, we reached the camp.

October 4.—The next day was showery, and we spent the morning about the flats, where the tracks of a bear that had passed along the edge of the woods the night before invited the hope of seeing it. Crossing the creek we circled through the woods to find a route up the mountain, and went some distance up the slope on the edge of a deep canyon, formed by a creek of fair volume dashing down from precipices near the crest. Across the canyon, not far above the bottom, we watched for some time a doe peacefully browsing.

October 5.—The *Iowa* had arrived shortly after we reached camp, bringing mail and newspapers, which occupied us the next morning while the rain again poured down and continued all through the day. After lunch we forced our way through the woods and dripping huckleberry bushes, and tramped on the prairie almost to the lower bight, but saw nothing except deer tracks and one old bear track. It was quite evident bears do not frequent these prairies very much, since the only signs I saw in them were the trails to the salmon creeks.

October 6.—It rained hard all the next morning while we walked about the flats without seeing any signs of bears, and after lunch we started in the boat for the creeks in the lower bight. The rain had slackened, the sky was heavily overcast, and a dense fog hung over the woods. A mink was playing about the smaller creek, which still contained a few salmon, but the direction of the wind was unfortunate, and no bear appearing before dark, we returned to camp.

The salmon creeks are at the head of the lower bight, and since the wind blows, unobstructed, almost continually from the east, it is a waste of time to watch these for bears which, before reaching the creeks, would be sure to receive one's scent. Those in the upper bight are more favorable, since they flow through clearings which extend north and south in the woods, and the wind there blows as often down the creeks as up.

October 7.—The stars were out in the night, but our hopes for the next day were dashed by a severe rain which lasted until late in the afternoon. Nevertheless we started to find a route up the mountain, southwest of camp, on which we had seen the two bears feeding in the saddle near the top. Going to the head of the bight, we walked through the woods half a mile to the canyon and began the ascent along its edge. Soon a doe jumped up a short distance ahead of us, and after looking at us a few moments, she walked upward, pausing now and then to look back, until she disappeared. After ascending to a point where the slope was too steep to climb, we turned and worked east, gradually rising, but without discovering any place where the mountain-top could be gained. The slope was full of creeks flowing over muddy ground, where the devil's-club was massed, and on the higher parts the whole surface, even under the trees, was covered with dense huckleberry bush and alders, all growing downward. At last I found what appeared to be a practical route to the top and, drenched as we were, the attempt to gain it was made.

A few short stretches were almost perpendicular, and the rest of the slope was so steep and slippery that we could only climb by zigzagging and holding on to the alders for support. Deer tracks became more numerous as we progressed higher, but no bear tracks were seen anywhere in the woods above the lower country. About two in the afternoon, rain mixed

with soft snow fell heavily, the sky grew dark, and
fog began to settle. Although we were within two
hundred yards of the top we decided that it was wise
to retrace our steps at once, as nothing could be
gained by continuing the climb except an encounter
with the cold wind, which was blowing very strong
above the timber.

On our return, soon after reaching the canyon, we
were at the foot of the cascades which dashed over a
series of cliffs several hundred feet high, all enclosed
in the dense woods. The roar was intense, and we
noted with interest a fine doe feeding in the salmon-
berry bush directly below, in the bottom of the canyon,
almost at the edge of the rushing water. After watching her for some time, I shouted and threw large sticks
and rocks toward her, but it was only after many attempts that I succeeded in frightening her enough to
cause her to move. The sides of the canyon were practically perpendicular, and evidently the doe felt secure
from any attack. At last she leaped up on a rock rising above the torrent, and a second leap brought her
to the bank opposite to us, which she began to climb.
Then followed a sight which revealed to me the wonderful capacity of those deer for adapting themselves
to their habitat. When one sails up to Alaska through
the inland passage, and finds that deer are abundant
on nearly all the islands, he assumes that they do not
frequent the steepest slopes of the ridges and mountains, since most of them appear to be practically
perpendicular. This deer, however, ascended a long
perpendicular slope with an ease and a rapidity at once

surprising and significant. She simply zigzagged her way by placing her legs around the alders or small trees and pulling herself upward while retaining a secure footing in the deep moss which covered the surface. After a short time she paused to feed on the small salmon-berry bushes scattered all about, and gradually fed upward until lost to sight. Doubtless all the deer of the coast region are as much at home on the steep slopes as in other places. Rain had defeated a hunt on the mountain-top, but we had found a route of ascent!

October 8.—Dawn ushered in a beautiful clear day, with a light wind blowing from the north. The mountains at the head of the basin were clear, and there was a good chance to see the slopes through my field-glasses. In a large area of green grass not far below the crest, at the very head of the basin, I saw distinctly a black hulk moving about. It was a bear feeding, but too far to hunt from our camp. It was at least five miles distant, with the woods intervening, and we could not even tramp up there and back during the short hours of daylight, from seven in the morning to five in the afternoon. The weather was too uncertain to move the camp up there, since we could not hunt high on the mountains during the rain and fog, and besides, we were obliged to leave the following week.

We started in the boat for the head of Pybus Bay, five miles distant. I wanted to see if the conditions there were favorable for hunting bears. Williams, who had daily remained in camp, had consumed great quantities of our venison; some portions of it had been given also to the men on the *Iowa*. Our stock of meat was low and we wanted another deer. Shortly after rounding a point opposite camp, we saw a doe and fawn feeding on the beach among some rocks. Mrs. Sheldon fired four shots from a distance of a hundred yards, but the boat was unsteady and the doe, followed by the fawn, walked off into the woods.

We reached the head of the bay at low tide and walked out upon vast flats teeming with ducks, geese, gulls, eagles, and ravens. Great meadows border the woods; a small salmon stream enters in the west arm, and another larger one in the east arm. . Low ridges are near on both sides, but the high mountains are many miles distant. Few bear signs were at the mouths of the creeks, nor did the pools contain any salmon. At the head of Pybus Bay the bears must seek the salmon far up the creeks, nearer the mountain ranges. I knew at once that there was no chance to see bears there. We spent most of the day looking for deer, and Williams took his boat across the bay to watch the beach on the east side. No deer were seen, and we started in time to reach camp before dark. The sunshine had brought hope and new ambition for the few days that remained.

October 9.—The stars shone that night, while the west wind was a favorable sign for the next day, which did not disappoint us. It was calm, with a cloudless sky, a typical Indian-summer day, like those in northern New England. A heavy frost had fallen during the night, the lake at the head of the bight was frozen, the mountains were glistening white, and the woods

Gulls at head of Pybus Bay.   October 8.

Lunching near head of Pybus Bay.   October 8.

for the first time *were dry*. As we climbed the precipitous slopes of the mountain and fought our way
upward through devil's-club, alder, and huckleberry bush we contrasted this with our last effort,
when we had soaked ourselves while climbing those
same slopes as the rain poured and the brush dripped!
The last hundred yards was up a ledge over which a
creek ·had carved out the rock almost into steps.
Though the surface was nearly vertical, we found a
footing and reached the top at eleven in the morning.

The crest almost overhung the bight below, where
all the islands appeared in miniature, the tide was high,
and the ripples made by the ducks in the water were
clearly visible. Away to the west and north stretched
the rugged ranges of Admiralty Island, while the
mountains of the basin, enclosing the forest-clad areas,
loomed up near and imposing. The top of the mountain was like a broad and rolling prairie; the surface
hard; here and there was a stunted pine, and in the
more level spaces were tiny ponds.

We took a westerly course, and reaching a convenient spot, near where the bears had been seen feeding
in the saddle, rested for a while to watch. Bald eagles
soaring along the crest were numerous, and once I saw
two ravens fighting one of them. I had for some time
noticed that, during that season on Admiralty Island,
the bald eagles uttered their screams only when they
perched on trees. That day I occasionally saw the
eagles, which were soaring along the crest, alight in
trees and begin at once to. scream, even when their
mates were still circling about them. Later we walked

west and soon saw a doe which I tried to photograph,
while a short distance beyond was another doe with
two fawns. As we approached, they walked to the
edge and went down the slope into the timber. Deer
tracks were very abundant near and on the top, but
we did not care to shoot one and risk the possibility
of frightening a bear.

Arriving at the western edge of the mountain, all
the glory of a marvellous landscape was before us.
Below was Pybus Bay with its islands, reefs, and in-
dented shores surrounded by timbered ridges. Beyond
was Frederick Sound, the most picturesque country
of the inland passage between Juneau and Seattle.
The lofty rugged mainland ranges, all snow-white, extended up and down the coast as far as the eye could
reach—a sea of peaks piled in bold outline above their
dark, timber-clad slopes. To the south, Kupreanof
Island rose out of the sound in dark, rolling timbered
ridges, and below us in that direction was the basin
of the lower bight, surrounded · by rough mountains
with serried crests, which presented a strong contrast
to the smoother mountains enclosing the basin above
our camp. While the sky was clear above and the
sun was pouring down cheerful warmth we seated ourselves on some soft, dry moss on the western edge
of our mountain, which divided the two basins, and ate
our lunch. Our enjoyment of the landscape before
us on that perfect day repaid us for all the storm, rain,
and disappointment we had endured before.

At three in the afternoon we returned to the saddle
and watched the grassy slopes, until lengthening

"The crest almost overhung the bight below."   October 9.

East end of bight and Pybus Bay from top of mountain.   October 9.

shadows warned us it was time to return. No bear appeared, nor did my field-glasses reveal one anywhere else on the mountains. As the ground on the top was too hard and mossy to receive impressions of bear tracks, I could not read any of their signs. We reached camp at dark.

October 10.—The next day was heavily overcast and showery. Once, when the clouds lifted at the head of the basin, I saw a bear, probably the one that had appeared before, in the same grassy area on the slope. A weasel that had been inhabiting our tent and feasting on our meat, finally stepped into a trap and I preserved its skin.

October 11.—During the night the southeast storm descended and lasted until two in the afternoon, when we started for the flats. I had again seen that bear feeding on the same place at the head of the basin, and now, finding no fresh sign about the flats, was confirmed in the belief that our only chance to find a bear was to climb the high mountains and look for one above the timber; but that required reasonable weather.

October 12.—A severe storm kept us in camp all the next morning until noon, when the rain stopped for a short time, during which I again saw the bear feeding at the head of the basin. Facing the rain in the afternoon, we went to the creeks and then walked about the west end of the flats, but saw nothing. One thing, however, interested me. Not long before dark several flocks of ducks came flying from the very head of the north indentation of the flats, followed immediately after by about a hundred geese. I knew that something had disturbed them, and looking through my glasses, saw a doe walking along close to where they had been feeding. I had not known before that a deer would thus frighten ducks and geese. We walked in that direction, but before we could reach the spot the deer took to the woods, and darkness descending rapidly, we groped our way back to camp.

October 13.—Our hopes sank when the rain was still falling the next morning, and we were obliged to give up ascending the mountains. We saw a deer swimming across the upper end of the bight, but it soon disappeared in the woods. Williams took us in his boat to the lower bight, and finding no salmon in the creeks, we took refuge in the woods against a southeast storm of wind, rain, and hail. All the gulls and eagles had left the bight. The storm constantly increased, and we began to doubt if Williams could bring his boat back.

After eating some lunch, we started back through the woods, toward the prairie. Soon I dimly descried a fine buck as it stood looking at us through the dense brush, forty yards away, and Mrs. Sheldon missed a snap-shot at it. As we reached the prairie, a doe was feeding a few yards ahead, but we did not molest it. Shortly I saw another buck, fifty yards below, in thick huckleberry bush, its hind-quarters toward us as it turned its head to gaze. In the brush it was a difficult mark, as the rain poured and the wind blew, and Mrs. Sheldon again missed. A second doe appeared a little later, but my companion did not shoot at it. The bucks had begun to move down off the higher ridges and the rut was about to begin.

Looking across Pybus Bay from mountain-top.   October 9.

Looking down on Frederick Sound from mountain-top.   October 9.

In rain and storm we accomplished successfully a three-mile tramp over the prairie, and the boat having arrived, we boarded it and reached camp some time after dark.

October 14.—As the steady downpour continued all the next day we could only hunt the prairie behind camp, in the hope of killing a deer. We tramped nearly to the lower basin when I saw a small buck as it disappeared in the brush. We saw a doe later, but did not kill it. Like the deer in Vancouver Island, we found those on Admiralty Island exceedingly tame, as are all the coast deer of British Columbia and Alaska, even in the places where they are much hunted. If the wind is right, they usually stand and look, even after seeing the hunter approaching. When they run, they put up their tails, as do the white-tail deer elsewhere.

October 15.—The next day was rainy and foggy and we spent all of it on the prairie without seeing a deer.

October 16.—The rain had stopped, there was no wind, and now and then a patch of blue sky appeared. In the early hours of the morning we had climbed to the top of the mountain, to be greeted by a doe innocently looking at us a few yards away. We did not disturb it, as, gradually retreating, it stopped every few steps as if to assure itself of our presence. All day long we ranged over the mountains, enjoying the landscape and watching vainly for bears. We reached camp just before dark to find the *Iowa* anchored near.

October 17.—Early in the morning we loaded our equipment and embarked. My disappointment was keen. Mrs. Sheldon's enthusiasm had been sustained undiminished, and her eagerness to kill a bear had constantly increased. Through rain and storm, contending with all the difficulties of that rough wilderness, she had eagerly endured the hard work necessary for success, but the weather had defeated her. In spite of that, it was with great regret that we sailed away from our little camp at the edge of the dark forest. Through stormy weather, in a heavy sea, we coasted along all day, and reached Juneau late at night. One very interesting and significant incident had occurred. As we were forcing through a heavy tide-rip, *three miles* off shore, two deer—a buck and a doe— were seen swimming. They were headed across Frederick Sound for the mainland, *nine miles distant*. Evidently a distance of ten or more miles of intervening water is no obstacle for these coast deer! Dickinson shot both and brought them to Juneau.

Our hunting trip had ended. Notwithstanding the weather, the experience had been delightful, and the wilderness had fastened its charm on both of us.

Admiralty Island, including also Baranof and Chichagof Islands, which are strictly similar in topography, offer the most attractive possibilities for bear hunting of any of those on the Alaska coast. The former is the most accessible, and bears are equally abundant there. The climate is practically the same, as well as the difficulties of travelling through the woods. The features of lofty mountain landscape are lacking in the Queen Charlotte Islands, and are somewhat subdued on Vancouver Island, where they cannot be at all enjoyed because of keeping to the forest in which the wapiti roams. The scenery of Admiralty is similar to that of Montague Island. Both contain high, rugged mountain ranges. From the mountain-tops of the former one can view the grandeur of Frederick Sound, from those of the latter the glories of Prince William Sound. Admiralty has many bays all around its coast line, all good harbors, and the constant sight of deer, which do not exist on Montague Island, gives added zest to the hunt. Water-fowl are more abundant along its shores. The Eskimos paddling the bidarkas are not there, but a few Indians from Juneau hunt and camp along the east coast, while those from the larger village of Killisnoo, on the west coast, hunt the western beaches. Bear hunting on Montague Island is limited by doubtful transportation along its east coast. A gasoline launch can be navigated all around Admiralty, and lie at anchor in the calm waters on the bays near where the bears must be hunted.

But anywhere along the Alaska coast, mainland or inland, spring is the only time to hunt them, not fall. To be sure, it is a wonderful sight to see the huge bear suddenly appear on the bank of a creek swiftly flowing through the great forest, while the salmon fight and splash and the gulls scream in plaintive voices as they hover about the pools. To see the bear leap into the rapids, sweep out a salmon with its paw, and retire silently into the wood to make its feast must be a stirring experience and one that would give a wonderful glimpse of wild life in the forest of the wilderness. It is, however, a field for the photographer, not the sportsman. A hunter of some experience could easily shoot several bears along the salmon creeks in September. But their pelage is light—hardly satisfactory as a trophy. There is little sport in hunting them by stealth, trusting to snap-shots in the brush, or watching silently until they come into the water, only to indulge in marksmanship and get the shot without effort. My experience on Montague Island is a description of what can be enjoyed on Admiralty Island during the month of May; for the habits of the bears on both are strictly similar, and they must then be stalked high up on the slopes above timber, while the wonderful landscape is unfolded before the vision.

The next day we sailed up the Lynn Canal, spent a day or two in Skagway, and then went over the White Pass Railroad to Whitehorse, where the sharp, cold air, the view of the mountains of the interior, the sweeping current of the Yukon waters, awakened crowding memories of my former days in the wilderness of those subarctic lands.

Returning to Skagway, we soon sailed down the inland passage, made short visits in Vancouver and Victoria, after which, having reached Seattle, we boarded the train and arrived in New York November the fourth.

Including the time spent in Nuchek, Ketchikan, and Juneau, I had spent among the coast islands, during the hunting trips described in this book, one hundred and forty days. Of this number, only twenty-seven full days and nine half days had been sufficiently free from rain and fog to permit of reasonable hunting.

Salmon running up creek which enters bight near our camp on Pybus Bay.
By permission of U. S. Geological Survey.

Any one who attempts to hunt in these islands in the same months must expect similar weather, though possibly in spring the rainfall on Admiralty might be slightly less than it was on Montague.

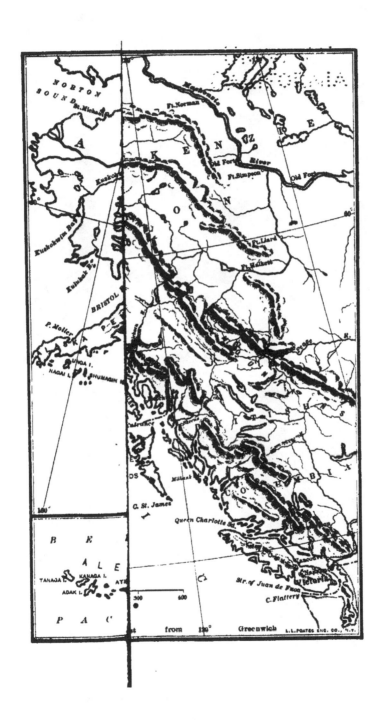

APPENDIX A

URSUS SHELDONI, A NEW BEAR FROM MONTAGUE ISLAND, ALASKA *

BY C. HART MERRIAM

SINCE it is not likely that my work on the American bears will be completed during the present year, it seems desirable to place on record the description of a large and remarkable new species from Montague Island, Alaska, of which five specimens of both sexes and different ages were obtained in May, 1905, by Charles Sheldon, and three additional specimens in 1908 by Miss Annie M. Alexander, all of which have been generously placed at my disposal for study.

Montague Island lies in the western part of the mouth of Prince William Sound, in latitude 60 degrees, only about 20 miles distant from the east shore of Kenai Peninsula—the home of *Ursus kenaiensis*. It is not surprising, therefore, that the Montague Island bear proves to be related to *kenaiensis*. The two together form a group quite apart from all the other known species.

It is peculiarly fitting that the Montague Island bear should be named in honor of its discoverer—Charles Sheldon, of New York—who by zeal and perseverance in the face of many obstacles succeeded in killing five, and generously presented the specimens to the U. S. Biological Survey.

The new bear may be known from its only near relative, *Ursus kenaiensis*, by the following description:

* Proceedings of the Biological Society of Washington, vol. XXIII, pp. 127-130, September 2, 1910.

Ursus Sheldoni sp. nov.

Type.—No. 137,318, ♂ ad., U. S. National Museum, Biological Survey Collection. Montague Island, Alaska, May, 1905. Charles Sheldon. Original number 17.

Characters.—Size large; claws of adult long and of the grizzly type; hairs over shoulders elongated to form a small but distinct hump; ears dark, with whitish tips; general color brownish, varying from pale to dark, the hairs of the back sometimes yellowish tipped, those of the head grizzled; color darkest (almost blackish) on belly, legs, and feet. An old she bear killed by Sheldon, May 18, 1905, is very pale grizzled gray on the upper parts, and only moderately darker on the legs and feet. The cub of this bear, killed the same day, was in its 2d year (about 16 months old) and is very pale—almost buffy gray— with dark feet and legs and a strongly marked hump.

Cranial Characters.—Skull in general similar to that of *kenaiensis* but basisphenoid broader and flatter, its length nearly equal to that of basioccipital; posterior roots of interpterygoid fossa more widely spreading; *condyle of jaw more exserted* [in *kenaiensis* sessile], reaching so far back that a line dropped from peak of coronoid to tip of angle touches or traverses it [in *kenaiensis* this line passes freely behind the condyle]; coronoid, in females of same age, smaller and lower—its area for muscular attachment less; ramus of jaw strongly bellied posteriorly, its inferior border below the coronoid *strongly convex downward* and curving evenly, with only a very slight break, to angular process. [In *kenaiensis* the inferior border of ramus is *nearly straight* (*not* appreciably bellied under coronoid) and ends abruptly in a step or jog at some distance behind the angle.]

In general form and appearance skulls of females closely resemble those of female *kenaiensis*, differing chiefly in the characters above mentioned and in certain dental peculiarities— notably the smaller size and more pointed heel of the last upper molar, and the oblique truncation of the 1st upper molar.

Skulls of males differ widely from those of *kenaiensis*. Only two full-grown males of *sheldoni* and one of *kenaiensis* are available for comparison.* The two adult ♂ skulls of *sheldoni*, while full grown, are by no means so old as the old male *kenaiensis*, compared with which they are decidedly larger (averaging 2 inches longer), much higher, more massive, broader across the squamosals and also across the frontals (both interorbitally and postorbitally). The ramus of the jaw is decidedly broader, and its inferior border more bellied and convex posteriorly. The sagittal crest does not reach the frontals [in the old ♂ *kenaiensis* it reaches to *middle* of frontals]; the frontals arch well upward, are traversed by a broad median sulcus, and swollen above and behind the orbits; the nasals are broad and long (in the type specimen reaching plane of postorbital processes).

Dental Characters.—Teeth in general of the grizzly type. Last (4th) lower premolar normally with horizontal heel, slightly upturned at posterior end, and shallow median sulcus reaching from cusp to end of heel, its defining ridges ending in slightly developed posterior cusplets. [In *kenaiensis* the last lower premolar is more conical, the heel sloping, the sulcus incomplete, with only a single posterior cusplet—on inner side of main cusp posteriorly.] First upper molar peculiar, having both ends *obliquely truncate and parallel*, sloping strongly from outer angles backward and inward; inner row of cusps pushed back so that each falls behind plane of corresponding cusp on outer side; the tooth as a whole more rectangular, its inner

---

* Those of *sheldoni* are the type, No. 137,318, collected by Sheldon in 1905; and a slightly older male of approximately the same size (No. 970, Mus. Vert. Zool., University of California), collected and loaned by Miss Annie M. Alexander (killed by her hunter, A. Hasselborg, July 31, 1908, at McLeod Harbor, Montague Island). The old male *kenaiensis* (No. 8946, Museum Vert. Zool., Univ. Calif.) was collected by Andrew Berg for Miss Annie M. Alexander, to whom I am indebted for the privilege of comparing it with skulls in the Biological Survey collection. It is very old and presents the maximum development of crests and ridges—the sagittal crest being very long and high, slightly convex, and reaching anteriorly to middle of frontals—the temporal ridges spreading thence at a right angle to the postorbital processes.

corners squarer (less rounded), and inner side more flattened and much less convex than in *kenaiensis*.

In the females the last lower molar is conspicuously smaller than in *kenaiensis*, and the last upper molar is smaller, narrower, more wedge-shape, and more pointed posteriorly. In one of the males it is similar. In the three other males the last upper molar is larger and less acute posteriorly than in the females, and the 3d cusp on the inner side is better developed.

Skull Measurements.—Following are measurements of two adult males—the type specimen collected by Sheldon, and a slightly older male collected by Miss Annie M. Alexander (No. 970, Museum of Vertebrate Zool., Univ. Calif.). In each case the measurements of the type come first, followed in parenthesis by those of the Alexander skull. Basilar length, 360 (355); zygomatic breadth, 270 (272); occipito-sphenoid length, 110 (104); postpalatal length, 163 (165); least interorbital breadth, 102 (99); distance from foramen magnum to plane of front of last upper molar, 242 (235); length of upper molariform series, 72 (75); of upper molars, 57 (61); of lower molars, 71 (72).

Remarks.—The skull of *Ursus sheldoni* is large and massive, and contrasted with those of the big bears of other parts of Alaska (*gyas, middendorffi, dalli*) is short and remarkably broad. The breadth is most conspicuous across the squamosals and frontals. Even the nursing cub shot by Sheldon has the skull strikingly broader throughout than any other cub in the collection. [I have not seen a cub of *kenaiensis*.] Skulls of females are flattened like those of *kenaiensis*. Skulls of males are high and rounded, and those approaching maturity—say in the 4th and 5th years, and doubtless for several years later—have the brain-case and frontals so elevated and swollen that were it not for the snout the skulls would appear almost globular.

Another curious feature is that as the skulls lie in a row on the table, those of *sheldoni* have the nose *conspicuously* tilted up. In females the actual difference in height of tips of nasals (above the table) is 8 or 10 mm.; in the males, 35–45 mm. This appears to be due to two causes—the more exserted condyle of *sheldoni*, which throws the jaws a little further forward, and the more bellied basal part of the ramus, which tilts the front part of the skull upward.

It is interesting to note that the 4th lower premolar is distinctly of the grizzly type, while in *kenaiensis* it is variable.

The material on which *Ursus sheldoni* is based is ample to show the constancy of the characters by which the species differs from all other bears. This material consists of 2 adult males, 2 young males (4 or 5 years old), 3 adult females, and 1 cub of the 2d year (about 16 months old).

APPENDIX B

THE following brief description of habits of this bear is based on my own observations (some of which are already recorded in the narrative) and information, which I considered reliable, gathered from the natives.

Bears do not go into hibernation before November, and sometimes, if the cold season is not advanced, until December. Their dens are usually made among the rocks above timber, and sometimes in large holes dug into the surface of the mountain slopes. They leave their dens about the first of May, or earlier if warm weather appears, when all, including those which hibernate in the western water-shed of the island, come immediately to the basins of the eastern water-shed, because the western side is covered with deep snow.

They begin at once to feed on a special grass, which, growing high above timber, has a reddish tip. Other grasses, growing both above and below timber, are much more abundant, but the bears do not touch them. At the same time they dig out and eat *microtus* mice. This red-tipped grass occurs only in certain parts of the basins, and grows most profusely in patches of ground favorably exposed to the sun for the early melting of the snow. The grass varies, therefore, in abundance. After leaving its den, the bear finds an area well supplied with this grass, and remains there for some time—three or more weeks, if the basin is well stocked with it; but if the supply is limited, after cleaning it out, the bear will go to the next basin. They browse on the grass in the same manner as cattle do.

I could find no evidence of bears attempting to dig out marmots, which have their burrows among the rocks. Mice are

exceedingly plentiful above timber as well as below, and the
bear always finds them at hand to supplement its vegetable
diet. It determines the underground position of a mouse by
scent, and digs, sometimes furrowing the earth along the mouse's
burrow, until the mouse is exposed, when the bear places its
paw over it, and, after biting it in the head, swallows it whole
without chewing it. It requires from five to ten minutes to dig
out a mouse, and a large proportion of those which the bear
attempts to capture, evidently running off before the bear can
place its paw over them, escape. The contents of the bears'
stomachs examined, indicated that the number of mice devoured
in a day seldom exceeds fifteen, and often less. For the first
three weeks after hibernation, bears do not eat very much and
their entrails are much contracted. There is little fat on the
bears during May, their flesh is still tainted with fish, and the
hair immediately begins to fall out, at first above the shoulders
and near the tail.

During the month of May they are diurnal, resting between
nine at night and six in the morning, and between nine or ten in
the morning and about four in the afternoon. They rest concealed, always at or above timber, and sometimes among alders
or stunted spruces high in the mountain slopes.

The bears are solitary, except in the case of twins or triplets
which remain together three or more years after separating
from the mother. The female bear may have one, two, or three
cubs, born during hibernation, and they remain with the mother
for two years, nursing her perhaps through the summer of the
second year, when they begin to get their food independently.

The last week in May the bears begin to travel widely, rang-
ing perhaps over the whole island, seeking more substantial
food. They often come to the beaches to eat dead fish, crus-
taceans, or whatever they can find. At any time after they
leave their dens, if a dead whale or seal is cast on the shore,
bears are sure to appear and feed upon them. In July all go
over to the salmon creeks on the west side to feed on the salmon
as soon as they begin to run, and there the bears remain until

the salmon are gone. Probably a bear or two go to the small salmon creek, entering the east side at the south end. During this time the bears also have a supplementary vegetable diet consisting of the roots of the skunk cabbage, *Lysichiton*, and berries when they can get them. I did not see any signs of bears digging the roots of skunk cabbage in May.

After the salmon disappear the bears clean up the dead, decaying fish, and then immediately repair above timber, eating a variety of grasses and mice, until they hibernate.

Trails which bears constantly travel over show a continuous series of single alternate footprints worn fairly deep into the soil, since each bear steps in the same track. Here and there, on the east side of the island, these trails lead from the basins down the creeks, but since the footprints are worn into the ground only where it is especially soft, the trails are much broken—a fact which shows that bears do not walk on them very often. A trail, well defined in some places, faint in others, runs twenty or more feet inside the woods, continuously parallel with the east shore. Here, bears travel in early summer and late fall, depending on their sense of smell to direct them to any food which may be on the beach. Edmund Heller, who accompanied the Alexander expedition to Montague Island in 1908, advises me that there is a similar trail in the woods, near and parallel with the beach, on the west shore of the island. This habit of travelling as much as possible under cover demonstrates the bear's caution, which always increases when it leaves the higher country. Both in Alaska and Yukon Territory, I have observed that bear trails along the salmon rivers are always made well back from the bars, where the bears can walk without being exposed to sight.

The Montague Island bear is excessively shy and flees from the presence of man. It seldom relaxes its caution. Not only does it conceal itself when resting, and keep out of the open as much as possible in the lower country, but when travelling or feeding above timber-line, it continually keeps pausing to swing its head back and forth for the purpose of sniffing the air. The

bear's eyesight is perhaps a little dull—at least they do not depend upon it in the slightest degree for detecting danger. They
seem to look only after hearing something, and their hearing is
very keen. But more than anything else, they depend for self-
protection upon their sense of smell, and if the scent of danger
reaches their nostrils, they run at once without waiting to look
for the source of it.

When shot at before suspecting the presence of an enemy, the
bear, whether hit or not, seldom detects the direction from which
the shot has been fired. After a moment of confusion, while
attempting to find the point of danger, the bear begins to run
and often starts directly toward the hunter. This is particularly likely to be the case if the bullet whistles over the bear or
strikes objects beyond it. It often does the same when hit.
Most people have interpreted this as "charging," when really
the bear is only running away from what it believes to be the
direction of danger.

On receiving a wound, a bear's first instinct is to run into
timber for the purpose of concealment, but after travelling for
a short distance through the woods, it starts up a mountain to
reach some high spot, as inaccessible as possible, where it feels
secure from the danger. If not wounded badly, it often travels
over two or three mountains before resting. Wounded bears
always seek to escape if possible. The female bear with cubs
acts the same way, nor does she stop to protect the cub. If hit
vitally, bears easily succumb. I have not observed that they
are more tenacious of life than most of the other American game
animals.

The natives say that these bears rut in July, when the male
appropriates a female and remains with her, but I am uncertain
as to the accuracy of their observations on this point.

Compared with the abundance of brown bears on the mainland north of the Lynn canal, and on Admiralty, Baranof, and
Chichagof Islands, few bears exist on Montague. If the rapid
increase of population about Prince William Sound leads to
active hunting of these bears, they will soon become extinct.

The habits of all the brown bears, both on islands and main-land, except when varied to suit local conditions, are similar.

Nothing is more striking than the general similarity in nature, actions, appearance, and habits of both the brown bears of the humid coast region of Alaska and the grizzlies of the dry interior. The several species of both of these coast and inland bears differ more or less widely in size, anatomy, color, and claws, but no one can observe them in their natural habitats without realizing that all have descended from a common ancestor.

APPENDIX C

In the fall of 1911, Dr. Merriam visited Victoria specially for the purpose of examining the specimens of the Queen Charlotte Islands caribou, which, before mounting them, Mr. Francis Kermode, with a true interest in science, had held for his inspection.

THE QUEEN CHARLOTTE ISLANDS CARIBOU, *RANGIFER DAWSONI* *

BY C. HART MERRIAM

THE most striking characters of the species are small size, imperfect development of antlers, and absence or indistinctness of the usual color markings. Throat mane feebly developed, reaching from throat nearly to forelegs, longest in middle, longest hairs 6 in. (150 mm.).

Color and Markings in Fall Pelage (November).—Coloration remarkably uniform and pale throughout, the usual dark areas indistinct or absent. General body color drab; top of head from edge of nose pad to horns, pale drab chocolate; top and sides of neck pale drab gray varying to buffy whitish, followed on shoulders by darker drab, but without trace of "cloak"; shoulders, upper half of back to tail, and outer side of thighs drab; flanks grayish, with indication of dark horizontal band below (just outside of white of belly); fronts and outer sides of legs and thighs paler drab, melting gradually into grayish white of ankles; inner sides of legs whitish, without line of demarcation; upper side of tail drab, slightly paler than back; under side of tail whitish; rump patch absent, but sides of rump pos-

* Description based on the type and four other specimens in the Provincial Museum, Victoria, B. C., which I was allowed to examine by the courtesy of the curator, Mr. Francis Kermode.—C. H. M.

teriorly, below plane of tail, faintly paler than above; nose pad, lips, ring around eye, ears, chin, throat, and ankles whitish; no markings on feet or ankles, the whitish of these parts passing insensibly into the pale drab of the legs.

Young.—The young cow is a little more strongly marked than the adults: dark color of head reaching farther back (to occiput); back and rump darker; flank band slightly more distinct.

Antlers.—Small, short, and poorly developed, with little if any flattening of the brow or bez tines (or elsewhere), and few "points." Brow and bez tines with normally 2 prongs each, one of which is sometimes forked, making 3 points; trez tine rudimentary or absent; tip usually forked, sometimes 3 pointed.

The antler may be straight (as in the type) or curvèd strongly forward (as in the old bull with largest horns). In the type specimen it (right antler) measures 695 mm. in greatest length in straight line. In the old bull the left measures on the curve 36½ in. (928 mm.); the right 32½ in. (825 mm.). The single antler (left) found by Commander Hunt measures on the curve 35 in. (890 mm.).

Skull.—Small and light compared with neighboring species; orbital rim prominent, its upper part deeply emarginate (cut away anteriorly); orbital border of lachrymal markedly and rather acutely convex; frontals strongly depressed between centres of orbits, behind which they rise abruptly to form a conspicuous thickened median ridge; under jaw light and slender; angle feeble; coronoid light.

CRANIAL MEASUREMENTS OF OLD BULL[*]

Estimated length of top of skull . . . . 350 mm.
Greatest interorbital breadth . . . . 156 mm.
Least interorbital breadth . . . . 112 mm.
Diameter of orbit . . . . 50 mm.
Length of premaxillæ . . . . 85 mm.
Length of nasals . . . . 105 mm.

[*] Skull imperfect, the hinder part sawed off so that total and basal lengths cannot be obtained.

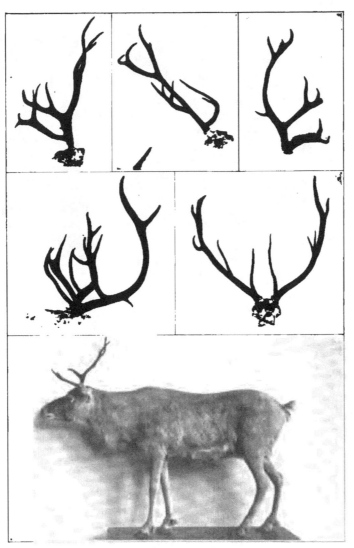

1. Type of *Rangifer dawsoni*—side view.   2. Type of *Rangifer dawsoni*—front view.   3. Left antler of *Rangifer dawsoni* collected by Commander Hunt.   4–5. Skull and horns of *Rangifer dawsoni* shot by Indians, November 1, 1908.   6. Mounted specimen of *Rangifer dawsoni* in Provincial Museum at Victoria, B. C.

Photographs by C. Hart Merriam.

Greatest breadth of nasals . . . .   52 mm.
Breadth of nasals anteriorly (opposite middle of maxillary) .   32 mm.
Front of premaxillary to maxillo-palatine suture . . . .   130 mm.
Tip of premaxillary to first tooth . . . .   98 mm.
Breadth of muzzle at posterior plane of premaxillæ . . .   67 mm.
Greatest breadth between molar series on outside . . . .   92 mm.
Greatest breadth between molar series on inside . . . .   60 mm.
Length of molar series of teeth, worn (6 teeth) about . . .   88 mm.
   [In the younger female, in which the teeth are only
      slightly worn, the same 6 teeth measure 93 mm.]
Length of mandible to back of condyle . . . .   280 mm.
   [Same in younger female, about 260 mm.]
Lower tooth row (6 teeth) on aveolæ . . . .   96 mm.
   [Length on tooth row (same 6 teeth) on crowns in the
      younger female, 100 mm.]

INDEX

(Scientific names of animals and birds, when known, are appended to the common name used in the text of the narrative.)